# CHRIST

## *in the Feast*
## *of Pentecost*

DAVID BRICKNER
RICH ROBINSON

# CHRIST
## *in the Feast of Pentecost*

MOODY PUBLISHERS
CHICAGO

Editor: Pam Pugh
Cover Design: DesignWorks Group Inc. (www.thedesignworksgroup.com)
Cover Images: Shutterstock

Library of Congress Cataloging-in-Publication Data

Brickner, David.
  Christ in the Feast of Pentecost / by David Brickner and Rich Robinson.
    p. cm.
  Includes bibliographical references and index.
  ISBN-13: 978-0-8024-1402-1
  ISBN-10: 0-8024-1402-8
  1. Pentecost Festival. 2. Shavuot. 3. Fasts and feasts in the Bible—Typology. 4. Typology (Theology) 5. Bible. N.T.—Relation to the Old Testament. I. Robinson, Rich. II. Title.

BV60.B75 2008
263´.97—dc22

                                                              2007032964

Choosing the person to whom we dedicate this book was an easy decision. Ruth Rosen has been a dear and trusted friend and colleague to both of us for longer than we choose to remember. She has through that friendship provoked us to think more incisively, to write with greater clarity, and to love the Lord more fervently. Ruth is very much the "wizard behind the curtain" of most Jews for Jesus publications, and though she has not often been given credit, we would like to acknowledge her profound contribution to this book, to our lives, and to the work of the Lord through Jews for Jesus. Thanks, Ruth! (Proverbs 27:9)

# CONTENTS

# FOREWORD

Scientists tell us that each person blinks on average twenty-five times every minute. Each blink takes only a fifth of a second. Therefore, if one takes a ten-hour journey, averaging a speed of only forty miles per hour, that person will have driven or ridden a total of twenty miles with their eyes closed. What a perspective!

As humorous as the above statement might be, what is not so pleasant is the lack of perspective so many have about how God has chosen to reveal Himself in history. Much can be missed by not having our eyes open along the fantastic journey of God's plan and purpose for His creation, the people of Israel, the Church of Jesus Christ, and His kingdom plan for history and eternity.

The relationship between the Hebrew Scriptures and the New Testament has been a debated topic for centuries. Continental divides of Bible students and scholars have been the result. Too many times in an attempt to navigate the channels of such studies boats have scraped and even crashed on opposite shores. The reality of the matter is that there is both continuity and discontinuity in the ways God has revealed Himself and His plan to work in history. This work is a valuable contribution to that discussion. All who read this book will be better for the experience and enriched by the diligent study of these two men. I know I won't read my Bible the same as a result of my read.

The purpose of this book is to shine a light on the Feast of Pentecost and its biblical significance. The authors of this book have done us a great service in putting some well-placed beacons along the banks of the channel for us to navigate through the waters of the roots of the Jewish faith from the Hebrew Scriptures, the traditional customs of Jewish practice, the significance of the life of Christ and the Church, and the ultimate fulfillment of Pentecost. As was the intended purpose of the Feast itself as it was commanded, there is a rich historical memory of what God had provided for His people, a present reality and responsibility for those with faith, and a future expectation that should both instruct and inspire us in our walk with God while waiting for the consummation of the kingdom and redemptive programs of God.

Mark L. Bailey
President
Dallas Theological Seminary

# GLOSSARY

**Akdamut:** acrostic poem in the Aramaic language, composed in the eleventh century by Rabbi Meir, praising God and picturing the Messianic future; recited during Pentecost.

**Akiva, Rabbi:** Second century rabbi famous for backing Bar-Kochba's rebellion against Rome 132–135 A.D. and declaring Bar-Kochba to be the Messiah.

**Atzeret:** "withdrawal, conclusion." A rabbinic name for Pentecost, suggesting that Pentecost concludes the season that began with Passover. The term is, however, used in the Bible in relation to the final days of Passover and Tabernacles.

**Aviv:** the older name for the spring month in which Passover falls; today called Nisan.

**Baitusim (Boethusians):** a group related to the Sadducees, or perhaps another name for the Sadducees themselves; they disputed the Pharisees regarding the correct date for Pentecost.

**Bar Mitzvah / Bat Mitzvah:** the coming-of-age ceremony for a boy at age thirteen (bar mitzvah) and for a girl at twelve (bat mitzvah).

**Bikkurim:** firstfruits.

**Challah:** a loaf of bread traditionally braided; used on Sabbath and other holiday occasions.

**Etz Chaim:** "tree of life."

**Gemara:** see *Talmud*.

**Hag ha-Bikkurim:** "Day of the Firstfruits," the name of Pentecost in Numbers 28:26–31.

**Hag ha-Katzir:** "Festival of the Harvest," the name of Pentecost in Exodus 23:16.

**Hag ha-Shavuot:** "Festival of Weeks," the name of Pentecost in Exodus 34:22, Deuteronomy 16:10, 16, which gives the holiday its most usual Hebrew name, "Shavuot" or "Weeks."

**Hasidim:** Plural of *Hasid*; ultra-Orthodox Jews, also known as *Hasidic* Jews; adjective, **Hasidic.**

**Kabbalah:** a system of Jewish mysticism that developed from medieval times onward. Kabbalah holds to ideas quite foreign to the Bible, such as reincarnation, and the idea that God exists in ten emanations (called *sefirot*—not to be confused with *Sefirat ha-Omer*). The chief textbook of Kabbalah is the *Zohar* (see that entry). Many Hasidim embrace the Kabbalah, and as a sort of Jewish "New Age" movement, it has enjoyed a recent resurgence in pop culture.

**Kalir, Eleazar:** medieval liturgical poet (also variously *Eliezer Kalir* or *ben Kalir*). His poems and hymns are often included in the prayers recited on various Jewish holidays.

**Ketubah** (plural, **ketubot**): a Jewish marriage contract.

**Lag Ba'Omer:** the 33rd day of the *omer* period; on this day the mourning practices that characterize the *omer* period are lifted.

**Manna:** the miraculous bread that God sent from heaven in the wilderness, first mentioned in Exodus 16:31.

**Mishnah:** see *Talmud*.

**Omer:** literally, a "sheaf"; originally referred to the sheaf offered as firstfruits, but today is more generally used of the entire forty-nine-day period between Passover and Pentecost.

**Oral Law:** Orthodox Judaism believes that along with the written Law (as found in the first five books of the Old Testament, the *Torah*), God also gave the inspired interpretation of the written Law. This interpretation was passed down orally until finally written down in the third–sixth century A.D.

**Pentecost:** "fiftieth," the Greek (and New Testament) name of the festival referring to the fiftieth day after the first day of Passover (Leviticus 23:16). Though today most Jews refer to the holiday by its Hebrew name of "Shavuot," older Jewish writers also often called it "Pentecost."

**Pogrom:** an organized, violent attack on Jewish communities, resulting in destruction of property as well as deaths. Mostly used of attacks on the Jewish villages (*shtetls*) of Eastern Europe over the past several centuries, but sometimes used of such catastrophes in other times and places.

**Reyzelakh:** papercuts designed to look like foliage or flowers; literally, "little roses."

**Sefirat ha-Omer:** the counting of the *omer* whereby each day of the *omer* period is counted off until its conclusion.

**Shavuot:** "weeks," the most common Hebrew name for the holiday.

**Simeon bar Yohai:** a student of Rabbi Akiva (see entry under *Akiva*) and the traditional (though not actual) author of the *Zohar* (see entry); mystically inclined Jews celebrate at his grave site on Lag Ba'Omer.

**Sivan:** the month of the Hebrew calendar in which Pentecost falls.

**Talmud:** the written compilation of commentary, legal discussion, and folklore that was produced from the third to the sixth century A.D. Orthodox Jews believe that the Talmud comprises the divine interpretation of the Torah (see *Oral Law*). The Talmud consists of two parts: the shorter *Mishnah*, compiled around 200 A.D., and the much longer *Gemara*, which exists in two versions, Babylonian and Palestinian, compiled third–sixth century A.D.

**Tikkun leil Shavuot:** the custom of staying up all night on the eve of Pentecost to study Scripture and traditional Jewish writings.

**Vilna Gaon:** Eighteenth century rabbinic sage who called for the abolition of using foliage during Pentecost as too close to Christian traditions; "gaon" literally means "genius" and was a title applied to a number of sages in Jewish history.

**Yiddish:** the language spoken by most Eastern European Jews from late medieval times on, related to German; now rarely used in daily life.

**Yom ha-Atzma'ut:** Israel Independence Day.

**Yom ha-Shoah:** Holocaust Remembrance Day.

**Yom ha-Zikkaron:** Memorial Day; commemorating Israeli soldiers who have fallen in war.

**Yom Yerushalayim:** Jerusalem Day.

**Z'man Mattan Toratenu:** "the season of the giving of our Law," a traditional Jewish name for Pentecost.

**Zohar:** central book of Jewish mysticism (see *Kabbalah*), actually originating in medieval times but traditionally held to be authored by Simeon bar Yochai in the second century A.D.

# A NOTE FROM
# THE AUTHORS

Some cross-cultural experiences "cross" to other cultures so successfully that people confuse their origins. Take, for example, the story of a friend who, for years, thought that Mah Jhong was a Jewish game. She had never seen a Mah Jhong set herself, and the only people she ever heard discussing the game were *bubbehs* (Jewish grandmothers). It was not until she had the opportunity to work with a Chinese American colleague that she discovered the true origin of Mah Jhong. That is not to say that all Jewish people mistakenly think that Mah Jhong originated in our culture. But this friend is probably not the only one who ever embarrassed herself by exclaiming to a Chinese friend, "Your grandmothers play Mah Jhong too?!"

The majority of Christians we meet realize that the Feast of Pentecost is a

Jewish holiday. But it is not surprising that some assume "Pentecost Sunday" is entirely Christian in origin. After all, doesn't Pentecost signify the birthday of the church? That doesn't sound very Jewish, does it? And if they have never heard Pentecost mentioned in its original (Jewish) context, why shouldn't they assume it is a purely Christian holiday? Unless they have Orthodox Jewish friends, they may never hear the holiday mentioned by Jewish lips.

Among less Orthodox Jews, Pentecost doesn't claim as much attention as some of the other Jewish holidays like Passover, Yom Kippur, Rosh Hashanah, or even Hanukkah. Though the Bible names the Feast of Pentecost as one of the "solemn feasts," it may seem to some like the poor stepchild of all the Jewish holidays. It is one of the "top three" Jewish holidays (as indicated by the fact that it required a special trip to Jerusalem), yet it remains the least understood and the least celebrated of them all.

The Festival of Passover has all the attraction and the elaboration of the ritual seder meal, focusing on Israel's deliverance from slavery in Egypt. The Festival of Tabernacles has the fun of building outdoor booths in which to celebrate, reminding us of our wilderness wanderings. Both holidays last for an entire week. Both are easily recognized by Christians as well-known Jewish holidays with special meaning for Christians, because of the things Jesus said and did as He celebrated them.

Pentecost, on the other hand, is a one-day celebration. Its rituals are not as widely known as those of Passover and Tabernacles. We have no record of Jesus doing or saying anything extraordinary during this feast. Although Pentecost may appear to be lacking by comparison in rituals and historical background, in reality, Pentecost is rich in meaning and has a depth of application. It touches on profound biblical themes and addresses subjects that are of utmost importance to the follower of Christ.

In this book, we will examine the ways in which this feast encourages us to be grateful as we give back to God and trust in His provision, as well as how it motivates us to study and learn God's Word.

We will begin with an overview of the Festival of Pentecost in the Old Testament. We will then see how the Jewish understanding of Pentecost gave birth to traditions that open our understanding of the New Testament celebration of the feast as well as how it is celebrated today. Next, we will examine the crucial role of Pentecost in the New Testament Scriptures. Finally, we will explore how Pentecost should inform our hopes and responsibilities (particularly for the work of missions and evangelism) until Christ returns.

In addition, we've provided what we hope will be good food for thought, including recipes for Pentecost, Scripture readings for personal devotions, and an entire Pentecost service for believers in Jesus.

We have gathered much information that is not new but, as far as we know, has not been brought under "one roof" to build your understanding of this holiday. We have reflected on the information to see what bearing it has on our own lives. We hope that this teaching will enrich and instruct God's people as well as show God's goodness and His offer of salvation to those who are searching for Him.

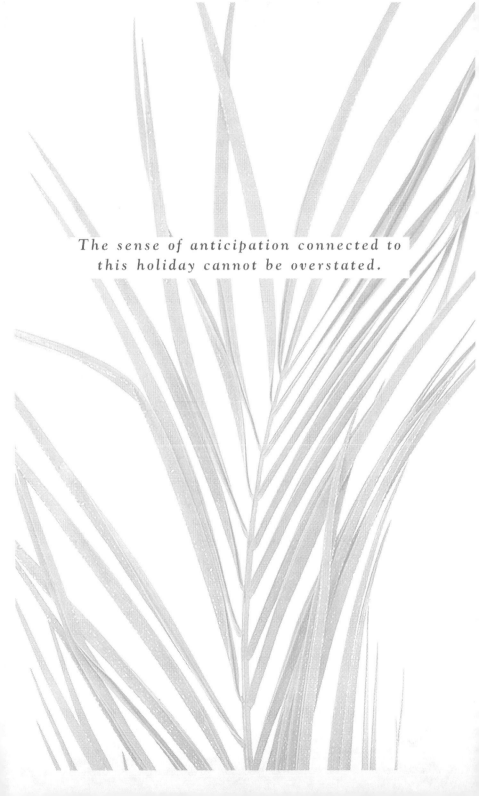

*The sense of anticipation connected to this holiday cannot be overstated.*

# Chapter One

# WHAT'S IN A NAME?

Names are important to God and so they should be to us. God, and sometimes people, frequently name individuals as well as places in accordance with their destiny, or to point out some aspect of their character. For example, God changed Abram's name to Abraham (Genesis 17:5) to reflect God's promise to make him the "father of many nations." Similarly, Abraham's wife Sarai was renamed Sarah ("princess"), undoubtedly to reflect her character as a "mother of nations" (Genesis 17:15–16).

Sometimes God gives a name that is not the name used in daily life; in 2 Samuel 12:24–25 the son of David and Bathsheba is named Solomon, the name by which he is known throughout the Bible; yet verse 25 says, "Because the LORD loved him, he sent word through Nathan the prophet to name him Jedidiah"—which means "beloved of the LORD." Likewise with places: when Jacob encountered God, "he called that place Bethel, though the city used to be called Luz" (Genesis 28:19; "Bethel" means "house of God").

Even so, the feasts of the Lord have meaningful names. The Bible often uses more than one designation to describe what happens during the holiday, as well as the themes and underlying significance of the celebration. In this chapter we will examine six names for the Feast of Pentecost, and the themes suggested by those names.

## 1. HAG HA-SHAVUOT

Have you ever noticed that one of the most challenging hours of the week comes just before you leave your home to attend a worship service? We rush about trying to get ready. Minor conflicts can become major crises and everything seems to take longer than expected. Imagine if getting ready for the worship service involved preparing for a journey that would take you far from home. Now imagine that not only you and your immediate family, but all your neighbors and friends are planning to journey with you, in a giant caravan of people heading off to worship. Preparation and planning would certainly set that worship service apart from the ordinary ones throughout the year. Such was the case with the Feast of Pentecost, which is best known in the Bible by its Hebrew name, *Hag ha-Shavuot*, or the Festival of Weeks.

(Note: If you mention this holiday to a Jewish friend, drop the "Hag ha" and use the name "Shavuot," which is how Jewish people refer to the holiday. Equally common among European Jews is the Yiddish pronunciation, "Shavuos.")

"And you shall observe the Feast of Weeks, of the first-fruits of wheat harvest" (Exodus 34:22 NKJV). The Hebrew word *hag*, in English "feast" or "festival," is related to the Arabic word *haj*, a familiar word in the practice of Islam. *Hag* implies a pilgrimage.[1] Pentecost was one of three festivals that required such a pilgrimage: "Three times in the year all your men shall appear before the Lord, the LORD God of Israel" (Exodus 34:23 NKJV).

The Hebrew word *shavuot* means "periods of sevens" or "weeks."[2] Yet the Feast of Weeks is not celebrated for weeks—or even one week. It is actually a one-day festival.

The name of the holiday does not describe the actual manner in which we celebrate it, as the Feast of Tabernacles does, nor does it point to the historical origin of the feast, as does Passover. Rather *Hag ha-Shavuot* is a chronological reference, pointing to the amount of time between Passover and this holiday.

God commanded the Israelites to count seven weeks from the day after Passover until the day when we are to celebrate this holiday, *Hag ha-Shavuot*. That is why the Bible calls it the Feast of Weeks.

"And you shall count for yourselves from the day after the Sabbath, from the day that you brought the sheaf of the wave offering: seven Sabbaths shall be completed. Count fifty days to the day after the seventh Sabbath; then you shall offer a new grain offering to the LORD" (Leviticus 23:15–16 NKJV; see also Deuteronomy 16:9).

The sense of anticipation or expectation connected to this holiday cannot be overstated. The holiday arrives as the climax of a season marked by a countdown beginning the day after Passover and lasting for seven weeks. This countdown emphasizes the theme of godly anticipation unique to this holiday. We don't count the days leading up to Passover nor do we count the days leading up to the Feast of Tabernacles. Pentecost, or the Feast of Weeks, is the only festival for which God commanded such a countdown.

Have you ever talked to a bride-to-be who is counting the days and hours until her wedding? Or to a student who is counting the days until summer vacation—perhaps even graduation? All the activities of life begin to organize themselves around this special time, and as anticipation for the event grows, people begin counting the days. That is the quality of expectation God built into this particular holiday as He required the children of Israel to count the days leading up to it. The famous rabbi Maimonides likened this exercise to someone who is waiting for their closest friend, counting the days and yes, even the hours.[3]

So as we think of the Feast of Weeks, we recognize that God intended for us to anticipate this celebration, to count, to expect—and that is one of the themes that will continue to unfold throughout our study of this festival.

## 2. HAG HA-BIKKURIM

A second name for the holiday is *Hag ha-Bikkurim*. You'll remember that "Hag" means festival or pilgrimage and "ha bikkurim" is Hebrew for the firstfruits.

"Also on the day of the firstfruits, when you present a new grain offering to the LORD at your Feast of Weeks, you shall have a holy convocation. You shall do no customary work" (Numbers 28:26 NKJV).

The Hebrew word *bikkurim* is related to the root word *bekhor*, which means firstborn. The idea of firstfruits is connected to the principle of the firstborn in Scripture. The Bible tells us that the firstborn of man and the firstborn of animals belong to God:

Consecrate to Me all the firstborn, whatever opens the womb among the children of Israel, both of man and beast; it is Mine. (Exodus 13:2 NKJV)

The Jewish tradition of *pidyon ha-ben*, the redemption of the firstborn, is based on God's claim in the above Scripture. In Numbers 3:40–51, we see that following the Exodus, God required a census and a price paid for every firstborn male of the children of Israel. This was a very practical way to demonstrate His claim to His people, helping them understand what they owed Him, and what He was willing to accept, by grace, instead. Even as Mary and Joseph brought the baby Jesus to dedicate Him in the Temple in Jerusalem (Luke 2:22), so we see throughout the Scriptures the firstborn were especially to be dedicated to God.

In the same way as God claims the firstborn, He tells His people that the firstfruits of the ground also belong to Him. Thus this festival of *Hag ha-Bikkurim*, Festival of Firstfruits, speaks to us of the importance of dedicating our first and our best to the glory of God.

Scripture promises a direct connection between our dedication and God's provision. "Honor the LORD with your possessions, and with the firstfruits of all your increase; so your barns will be filled with plenty, and your vats will overflow with new wine" (Proverbs 3:9–10 NKJV).

This passage and principle should not be used to raise false hopes that prosperity is attainable in proportion to what we give. It would be foolish to calculate one's giving based on what one expects to receive in return. Giving that is motivated by what one will receive is not giving at all. The key to this verse is to honor the Lord. When we recognize that all we have belongs to God, we honor Him. When we dedicate ourselves and the firstfruits of what He provides for His use, we honor Him. When we trust that giving our firstfruits for His special use will not leave us destitute, we honor the Lord. This leads to His blessing. He blesses us because we acknowledge that we and all we have are rightfully His, and He blesses us because in giving back firstfruits, we demonstrate our trust that He intends to continue to provide for us. This is instructive for all of God's children. Honoring the Lord with our firstfruits is part of the dedication and trust He expects and deserves.

## 3. HAG HA-KATZIR

A third name for the Feast of Pentecost is *Hag ha-Katzir*, which simply means the festival of the harvest. This is likely the earliest name given. We find it in Exodus 23:

> Three times a year you shall celebrate a feast to Me. You shall observe the Feast of Unleavened Bread; for seven days you are to eat unleavened bread, as I commanded you, at the appointed time in the month Abib, for in it you came out of Egypt. And none shall appear before Me empty-handed. Also you shall observe the Feast of the Harvest of the firstfruits of your labors from what you sow in the field; also the Feast of the Ingathering at the end of the year when you gather in the fruit of your labors from the field. (Exodus 23:14–16 NASB)

Most of us are far removed from an agrarian society such as the Israelites experienced during Bible times. Almost everything we eat has been at least partially prepared by someone else. But in ancient Israel the cycle of sowing and reaping was absolutely central to the existence of the Jewish people; it was part of the day-in, day-out rhythm of life. The

Feast of Pentecost was an important juncture in that cycle of harvest. It commemorated the ending of the barley harvest and the beginning of the wheat harvest in the land. The emphases of the harvest festival are the themes of God's provision and our gratitude to Him for His covenant faithfulness.

This gratitude and the joy that comes with it are central to another harvest festival, the Feast of Tabernacles.[4] In both harvest festivals God commanded the children of Israel to rejoice.

Leviticus 23:40 (NKJV) refers to the Feast of Tabernacles: "And you shall take for yourselves on the first day the fruit of beautiful trees, branches of palm trees, the boughs of leafy trees, and willows of the brook; and you shall rejoice before the LORD your God for seven days."

Deuteronomy 26:10–11 (NKJV) refers to the Feast of Firstfruits: "'. . . and now, behold, I have brought the firstfruits of the land which you, O LORD, have given me.' Then you shall set it before the LORD your God, and worship before the LORD your God. So you shall rejoice in every good thing which the LORD your God has given to you and your house, you and the Levite and the stranger who is among you."

Don't you love these commands to rejoice? The apostle Paul echoes and expands on them in Philippians 4:4: "Rejoice in the Lord always. I will say it again: rejoice!"

It may seem odd that God would have to command His people to be joyful. But which one of us does not get weighed down by the cares and the troubles and the woes of this world? We sometimes forget the things for which we ought to be grateful, and gratitude and joy go hand in hand. So God comes to us in His Word and through festivals like this and says, "Stop. Stop your preoccupation with the cares of life, stop with all the worries that weigh you down, stop and be happy about what you have, and for God's sake, have a good time!" A lot of people think of religion in general and Christianity especially as being a sour, dour, unhappy way to live. People have told us, "I don't want to follow Jesus because I'll have to stop having fun." If only they could understand God's heart for His people. He commands us to rejoice.

What is more, this rejoicing is a community event. It is not something that we're supposed to experience alone but with all of God's people. And we are supposed to remember where we came from. Remember that you were slaves in Egypt and do this. Remember that once you were strangers and aliens and so, God tells Israel, find some strangers, some aliens, and share some joy with them. This is what it means to rejoice. Showing grace to others who are in need reflects how you understand and appreciate God's grace in your own life.

Jewish tradition later added the reading of the book of Ruth as a ritual to celebrate this festival (see chapter 4). First, the events of the book take place during the barley harvest, making it a seasonal story, appropriate for the festival. More than that, Ruth was a stranger and an alien who received much kindness and grace from Boaz, a wealthy Israelite. Boaz, in accordance with Leviticus 19:10; 23:22, did not harvest the very full extent of his field in order to provide for Ruth and her mother-in-law, Naomi. Boaz was faithfully following God in this season of firstfruits. He showed gratitude to God by being gracious to others. Even so, our attitude toward others should reflect awareness of all God has done for us.

# 4. Z'man Mattan Toratenu

*Z'man Mattan Toratenu* means the season of the giving of our Law. This fourth name is not found in the Bible but was given by the rabbis. Exodus 19 provides a clue as to why the rabbis added this name to the Festival of Weeks.

In the third month after the sons of Israel had gone out of the land of Egypt, on that very day they came into the wilderness of Sinai. (Exodus 19:1 NASB)

The chapter goes on to describe the giving of the Law. The third month of the Hebrew calendar is called Sivan, and the Feast of Weeks falls on the sixth of Sivan. The rabbis concluded that this historical event happened in conjunction with the celebration of this feast we now call Pentecost. While the Bible doesn't give us the specific date when the Law was given, it is not at all unreasonable to believe the giving of the Law converged with this feast. We will return to discuss this point in greater detail when we come to the celebration of Pentecost as recorded in Acts 2. For now it is sufficient to say that in the Jewish community the giving of the Law at Mount Sinai has become integrally connected to the celebration of this harvest festival. This adds another theme to our study: the relationship between law and grace.

It is traditional, therefore, not only to read the book of Ruth but also the story of the giving of the Law in Exodus 19 and 20, including the recitation of the Decalogue, the Ten Commandments.

# 5. ATZERET

A further rabbinic title given to the festival is *Atzeret*, which has been translated "withdrawal," "conclusion," and "convocation." *Atzeret* is the most common word the rabbis use to refer to this festival, but in the Bible it is not actually used of this holiday at all. However, Scripture does use *atzeret* to refer to the last day of Passover and the eighth day of the Feast of Tabernacles. It is most commonly understood to mean a concluding convocation. Unlike Passover and Tabernacles, Pentecost is a one-day holiday, and as on the other two holidays, the Israelites were to withdraw from their regular work (see Leviticus 23:21; Numbers 28:26). The sages of Judaism used *atzeret* to refer to the one-day celebration because they didn't want to limit the celebration of the giving of the Law to just one day. They insisted that the Torah should be celebrated every day of the year, with a special concluding celebration at Pentecost. Therefore, in the Talmud, *atzeret* is the preferred name.

# 6. PENTECOST

The last name for this festival is best known among Christians. *Pentecost* is actually a Greek word meaning fiftieth. "Count fifty days to the day after the seventh Sabbath; then you shall offer a new grain offering to the LORD" (Leviticus 23:16 NKJV). This name for the festival, like the Feast of Weeks, once again emphasizes the idea of counting. Whether we count seven weeks or forty-nine days after Passover, we arrive at the same fiftieth day.

*Pentecost* is used in the Septuagint, the Greek translation of the Hebrew Scriptures, and so it became the common reference to this festival in both the Jewish and Christian communities.

There can be no doubt that the Feast of Pentecost was important to the early church, chiefly because the early church was a Jewish church. In Acts 20:16, Luke tells us Paul was hurrying to get back to Jerusalem, if possible, by the Day of Pentecost. In 1 Corinthians 16:8 Paul tells the Corinthians, "I will stay on at Ephesus until Pentecost," and so twice we see Paul making reference to his own schedule in keeping with this counting up to the Feast of Weeks.

Of course the greater significance for the church came as a result of what happened to the disciples on this feast day as it followed on the heels of Christ's resurrection and ascension.

"And when the day of Pentecost had come, they were all together in one place" (Acts 2:1 NASB).

There is no way to overstate the historic significance of what occurred in that room in Jerusalem. It forever changed this festival, making it a key date on the Christian calendar by adding an astounding new theme: the work of the Holy Spirit in the church, specifically in the arena of missions and evangelism. We will cover this in detail in chapters 6, 8, and 9.

Just as the Festival of Passover, with all its historic meaning, also pointed forward to the death and resurrection of Jesus, so the Feast of Pentecost pointed forward to another pivotal event in the history of the church. To truly appreciate what happened in that room, we should explore the rich background of the Old Testament festival in all of its fullness.

*We are part of a greater picture, on the road to greater events than we can imagine.*

# Chapter Two

# Pentecost in
# the Old Testament

## The Bigger Picture:
## Firstfruits

Of the three Old Testament pilgrimage holidays, Pentecost (Shavuot) stands out as the only one that the Bible does not link directly to a historical event.[1] Passover (Pesach) memorializes the exodus from Egypt; Tabernacles (Sukkot) recalls the wilderness wanderings; but Shavuot is linked to the agricultural cycle[2] and particularly to the harvest. As such, it is one of several firstfruits celebrations.

## Agriculture for Urban Dwellers

If you are a farmer, perhaps growing wheat in Kansas or citrus crops in California, you have an advantage in relating to a holiday centered on agriculture.

But if you grew up in an urban area, or even a suburban area, perhaps your eyes glaze over at the biblical mentions of sowing, harvesting, and reaping. How can the majority of us—who rely on people we've never met to grow our food—relate? We may be quick to thank God for our meals, but how many of us know what it takes to have a good harvest, and how many of us have felt the need to ask God, year in and year out, to bless the crops?

Imagine going to the local grocery store and seeing the produce department and many of the shelves practically bare. No fresh corn—the crops were eaten by insects. No cereal—the drought ruined the wheat. No grapefruit for your breakfast—the frost killed the citrus. No milk and no meat, because the cattle died from the same drought that ruined the wheat. The Food Network is canceled, and your favorite restaurants are going out of business because there is not enough food to eat, much less to use for entertainment.

If you've taken a moment to appreciate the challenges farmers have faced through the ages and the importance of agriculture that so many of us take for granted, you've just begun to scratch the surface of this holiday. There is far more to it than celebrating another year of good food and drink. Pentecost is a holiday rich in theology, and the firstfruits aspect offers spiritual lessons for us all.

## A LOOK AT THE CALENDAR

The theology of firstfruits and Pentecost is best understood within the context of the Israelites' agricultural year and the various firstfruit ceremonies.

In modern Hebrew, *aviv* means *spring*, and indeed Aviv begins in our March or April. The barley harvest ripens in early spring. By May or June (late spring), the wheat is ready for harvest. Summer brings figs, pomegranates, honey (which in the Bible generally refers to the "honey" of dates), and various nuts. Finally, in the fall, around September or October, grapes and olives are gathered. Winter alone holds no hope of a harvest.

## FIRST THINGS FIRST!

When each long-awaited harvest matured and ripened, it was reaped with great joy. Yet the crops were not ready for consumption. Before anyone could make bread, cake, or anything else from the crops, the first portion, or "firstfruits" (which includes more than a fruit harvest), was offered to God. There are two common terms for "firstfruits," *bikkurim* and *resheet* (both from roots meaning "first"; *resheet* also has implications of "choice or best").[3] *Bikkurim* became the more common word for firstfruits. This offering became food for the priests (they had no crops of their own, so various offerings or portions thereof essentially made up their salary). With the firstfruits properly offered and received, the farmer could use most of the rest of the crop (Leviticus 23:14). "Most" because a portion was also to be left for the poor (Leviticus 23:22) as well as for orphans, widows, and aliens (Deuteronomy 26:12).

The Scriptures highlight the firstfruit offering for each harvest season but do not specify from which particular crops firstfruits were to be brought. Later tradition mandated that firstfruits be brought only from certain crops known as the "seven species." These were the seven products of Israel mentioned in Deuteronomy 8:8: wheat, barley, grapes, figs, pomegranates, olives, and dates ("honey" in that verse refers to date honey). Firstfruits offerings in the time of Jesus would have consisted of one or more of these seven items.

One Israeli scholar has suggested that these particular crops are especially subject to the extremes of weather in Israel. Therefore, offering firstfruits from these crops challenged the Israelites (more so than giving offerings from other, hardier crops) to remain faithful to God, and trust Him through the difficult seasons.[4]

## EARLY SPRING HARVEST

When the first grains pushed up from the ground, a sheaf (*omer*) was to be brought to the priest, along with various other offerings as described in Leviticus 23:10–14:

> Speak to the Israelites and say to them: "When you enter the land I am going to give you and you reap its harvest, bring to the priest a sheaf of the first grain you harvest. He is to wave the sheaf before the LORD so it will be accepted on your behalf; the priest is to wave it on the day after the Sabbath. On the day you wave the sheaf, you must sacrifice as a burnt offering to the LORD a lamb a year old without defect, together with its grain offering of two-tenths of an ephah of fine flour mixed with oil—an offering made to the LORD by fire, a pleasing aroma—and its drink offering of a quarter of a hin of wine. You must not eat any bread, or roasted or new grain, until the very day you bring this offering to your God. This is to be a lasting ordinance for the generations to come, wherever you live."

## LATER SPRING HARVEST

Pentecost falls during this time. It occurs seven weeks after the early spring firstfruits, counting from "the day after the Sabbath" (discussed in chapter 3). The firstfruit offering for this offering is wheat, again to be accompanied by various other offerings.

And you shall count for yourselves from the day after the Sabbath, from the day that you brought the sheaf of the wave offering: seven Sabbaths shall be completed. Count fifty days to the day after the seventh Sabbath; then you shall offer a new grain offering to the LORD. You shall bring from your dwellings two wave loaves of two-tenths of an ephah. They shall be of fine flour; they shall be baked with leaven. They are the firstfruits to the LORD. And you shall offer with the bread seven lambs of the first year, without blemish, one young bull, and two rams. They shall be as a burnt offering to the LORD, with their grain offering and their drink offerings, an offering made by fire for a sweet aroma to the LORD. Then you shall sacrifice one kid of the goats as a sin offering, and two male lambs of the first year as a sacrifice of a peace offering. The priest shall wave them with the bread of the first-fruits as a wave offering before the LORD, with the two lambs. They shall be holy to the LORD for the priest. And you shall proclaim on the same day that it is a holy convocation to you. You shall do no customary work on it. It shall be a statute forever in all your dwellings throughout your generations. When you reap the harvest of your land, you shall not wholly reap the corners of your field when you reap, nor shall you gather any gleaning from your harvest. You shall leave them for the poor and for the stranger: I am the LORD your God. (Leviticus 23:15–22 NKJV; cf. Exodus 23:16; 34:22; Numbers 28:26)

## FALL HARVEST

Though the word "firstfruits" is not used, the text suggests that firstfruits were offered from this harvest as well. Among other things, those crops included olives and grapes.

> You shall observe the Feast of Tabernacles seven days, when you have gathered from your threshing floor and from your winepress. And you shall rejoice in your feast, you and your son and your daughter, your male servant and your female servant and the Levite, the stranger and the fatherless and the widow, who are within your gates. Seven days you shall keep a sacred feast to the LORD your God in the place which the LORD chooses, because the LORD your God will bless you in all your produce and in all the work of your hands, so that you surely rejoice. Three times a year all your males shall appear before the LORD your God in the place which He chooses: at the Feast of Unleavened Bread, at the Feast of Weeks, and at the Feast of Tabernacles; and they shall not appear before the LORD empty-handed. Every man shall give as he is able, according to the blessing of the LORD your God which He has given you. (Deuteronomy 16:13–17 NKJV)

## UNSPECIFIED TIMES

Scripture mentions other crops that ripened at various times without attaching them to a particular season or holiday. Numbers 18:12 mentions olive oil and new wine (normally associated with the fall harvest, though Numbers does not specify the season); Deuteronomy 18:4 mentions the first wool from sheep. Note that olive oil, wine, and wool are not raw materials; they represent the fruit of our hands as well as the fruit of nature. Compare Deuteronomy 16:15 cited above: "because the LORD your God will bless you in all your produce *and in all the work of your hands*, so that you surely rejoice." See also the chart on page 49 on the elements of the Leviticus 23 ceremony, under the first part, "two loaves." For firstfruits at unspecified times, see Exodus 23:19; 34:26; Leviticus 2:12, 14; Deuteronomy 26:1–10.

## TO SHOW GRATITUDE

Gratitude does not show itself merely in the joy with which we receive blessings but in our desire to give somthing back to God. Greedy people take as much as they can, but grateful people show their appreciation through giving. Bringing the first of the crops was an important way for the Israelites to show gratitude to God for His provision.

The theme of gratitude runs through all of Scripture, but the holidays provided a change of pace so that people would actually stop what they were doing to focus on thanking God. Passover expresses gratitude for redemption; Sukkot is about showing gratitude for God's provision during the wilderness wanderings. Pentecost was a time to express tangible thanks for the basics of life, and to emphasize that God was the ultimate Giver.

"Give us today our daily bread" (Matthew 6:11; see Luke 11:3). Jesus taught us to pray, and perhaps that prayer was a meditation throughout the year, as He saw worshipers streaming to Jerusalem with their baskets of firstfruits.

Shavuot and the other firstfruits occasions were more than gestures of thanks to God for His present provision. We are a people who do not live only for today; we have a *history* and a *destiny*. We look back to remember what God has done for us in the past, and we look forward to how He'll keep His promise to be our Great Provider in the future. Firstfruits illustrates that graphically.

Remember how God instructed the Israelites concerning what they should give upon entering the land God had promised to them (Leviticus 23:10). Perhaps that seems unremarkable, but remember that this command was given relatively soon after the Israelites had been freed from slavery in Egypt. They were on the first leg of a trip to the Promised Land of Canaan—a trip that some say could have been completed in less than a month. But as we know from the book of Numbers, the journey took forty years! Forty years—not because we didn't stop to ask for directions but because we rebelled against God, complained about His provision, and turned against His appointed leaders. Note the "we"—it is always a good idea when reading the Bible to think in terms of "we" rather than "they." Whether we are Jews or Gentiles, we need to apply the lessons to our own lives. The consequence of the *qvetching* (Jewish for complaining) was to wander in the wilderness for forty years. Forty years, by the way, is about the length of a biblical generation. It was the following generation—many of whom were the first generation born in freedom in over four hundred years —that entered into God's promises.

Here is what is remarkable. Although God punished the rebellious generation, He did not abandon them. He continued to provide direction (the pillar of cloud by day, the pillar of fire by night), sustenance (manna), and even extended wear on their sandals (see Deuteronomy 29:5).

Back to the words of Leviticus 23:9–10, which appear to have been spoken sometime between Exodus 19, when the Law was first given, and the end of Deuteronomy, when Israel was about to settle in the land. If we assume that during those forty years of wandering the Israelites discussed and repeated the Law among themselves, they would have heard the words of Leviticus 23 even as they wandered in the wilderness because of their sin. Yet God did not say, "*If* you enter the land" but "*When* you enter the land . . ." These words were a promise to the nation, and though that first generation did not live to see it fulfilled, the next generation did.

The God who acted in the Old Testament is the same God who became incarnate in Jesus the Messiah. His promises today are not just to a nation, but He has also made promises to a multinational body, the body of Christ, the church. We do well to remember that rebellion and ingratitude bring consequences. While God may exercise a measure of judgment, His promises remain steadfast.

## THE PASSOVER-PENTECOST CONNECTION

It is not exactly accurate to say that the Feast of Pentecost has no connection with a historical event. Later Judaism declared Pentecost to be the day on which God gave the Law to Israel. But we do not need to rely on tradition for a historical connection. The stipulation that firstfruits occurs seven weeks after Passover gives us a Passover-Pentecost linkage. But we find an especially strong historical connection in Deuteronomy:

When you have entered the land the LORD your God is giving you as an inheritance and have taken possession of it and settled in it, take some of the firstfruits of all that you produce from the soil of the land the LORD your God is giving you and put them in a basket. Then go to the place the LORD your God will choose as a dwelling for his Name and say to the priest in office at the time, "I declare today to the LORD your God that I have come to the land the LORD swore to our forefathers to give us." The priest shall take the basket from your hands and set it down in front of the altar of the LORD your God. Then you shall declare before the LORD your God:

> "My father was a wandering Aramean, and he went down into Egypt with a few people and lived there and became a great nation, powerful and numerous. But the Egyptians mistreated us and made us suffer, putting us to hard labor. Then we cried out to the LORD, the God of our fathers, and the LORD heard our voice and saw our misery, toil and oppression. So the LORD brought us out of Egypt with a mighty hand and an outstretched arm, with great terror and with miraculous signs and wonders. He brought us to this place and gave us this land, a land flowing with milk and honey; and now I bring the firstfruits of the soil that you, O LORD, have given me."

Place the basket before the LORD your God and bow before him. And you and the Levites and the aliens among you shall rejoice in all the good things the LORD your God has given to you and your household. (Deuteronomy 26:1–11)

This description of a firstfruits ceremony is not necessarily restricted to Pentecost, but certainly includes it as one of the firstfruits occasions. We can easily see how that ceremony connects firstfruits to the Exodus. (For that reason, this passage is included in the Passover Haggadah, the liturgy we use for that holiday.) Several aspects of this declaration can help us keep the events of our own lives in perspective:

*The declaration invokes history and puts us in the context of a story that is larger than we are.* The offering of firstfruits was not just to say thank You to God for a good year of crops. It was a way of remembering where we had been and where God had brought us.

Each of us has an individual history, but we also have a corporate history. We all were once unbelievers. Even if we were too young to remember when we came to faith, we all have a history of how God saved us, and of our life with Him since then. And, as part of the corporate church, we are all on a journey to the consummation of ultimate redemption when Jesus returns.

Perhaps you've read or seen the film version of the *Lord of the Rings*. Frodo Baggins, along with his companions, sets out on a journey to destroy the ring forged by the evil Sauron. They meet with all kinds of adventures and dangers, as well as various interesting friends. But the impact of the book hinges on the fact that, at each step of the way, the reader can see that the hobbits are *part of a larger story* of cosmic redemption.

So it was with Israel, and with us. We are part of a bigger picture, on the road to greater events than we can imagine. To thank God for a good crop is one thing. To thank Him because we recall how He delivered us, and because each year's crop is a link in a story leading up to a promise of final deliverance—that is something else!

*The Deuteronomy declaration also helps us to understand that the past is still **our** story.* The worshipers include themselves in the events of the story though they were not physically present at the Exodus (remember, this ceremony was to be recited generation after generation). The worshiper declares that "the LORD heard *our* voice and saw *our* misery . . . the LORD brought *us* out of Egypt. . . . He . . . gave *us* this land . . . the soil that you, O LORD, have given *me*." The ancient story is to remain *personal* in every generation.

At the annual Passover *seder* (ritual dinner) at which Deuteronomy 26:1–11 is recited, there is a section titled "The Four Sons" in which each sibling shows how he sees himself in relation to "the bigger picture." One son is wicked, because he does not include himself in what is happening. Instead, he asks, "What do these ceremonies mean that the LORD commanded *you* to observe?" Then there is the wise son, who *does* include himself: "What do these ceremonies mean that the LORD commanded *us* to observe?" (The remaining two are the simple son who knows no more than to ask, "What is all this?" and the son who is too young to ask anything and must be instructed.) Indeed, at the seder, we read that "in every generation one must look upon himself as if he personally had come forth from Egypt." Some Haggadahs from the fifteenth century actually illustrate that text with a picture of someone examining himself in a mirror—literally, looking upon himself![5]

James, too, suggests that applying the Scriptures to ourselves is like looking in a mirror.

Anyone who listens to the word but does not do what it says is like a man who looks at his face in a mirror and, after looking at himself, goes away and immediately forgets what he looks like. But the man who looks intently into the perfect law that gives freedom, and continues to do this, not forgetting what he has heard, but doing it—he will be blessed in what he does. (James 1:23–25)

By "looking" and applying what we read in the Bible to ourselves, we see that God's salvation story is not only the story of people who lived long ago—it is our story as well. Every lesson that Israel learned is a lesson that we need to remember for ourselves. The God whom Israel came to experience is our God as well. Likewise, when we read in the New Testament that Jesus died and rose again to take upon Himself the sins of the world, we are to realize that it is our sin that brought Him to the cross.

## IN THE PRESENT

Firstfruits and Pentecost connected us, not only to our *history* (redemption) but also to our *destiny* (partaking of God's promises). These occasions provided us with an opportunity to make the most of the present because of the following:

These occasions were opportunities to exercise **trust** and **faith** as opposed to self-reliance. The weeks between Passover and Pentecost were critical for the produce of the land. Typically in this region, hot southern winds and cold northern winds alternate one after another. The proverb "One man's meat is another man's poison" is no truer than in this period. The cold north wind is good for wheat but can destroy olives and grapes. The hot southern wind is beneficial for olives and grapes but can ruin the wheat and barley.

God promised that obedience would lead to blessings in the harvest, but that didn't mean that obedience would come easily or that the gamut of human emotions would disappear in the midst of trust. As seven weeks were counted off between Passover and Pentecost, we can imagine the farmer holding his breath with each passing day, hoping that the crops will not be ruined by a shift in weather. "Oh Lord, I believe—help my unbelief!" It must have been challenging to live a live of faith, not just once but each season, year in and year out, as the agricultural cycle repeated.

It is natural for human beings to trust something or someone, but we find it difficult to trust what we cannot see. Through much of the Old Testament, one of Israel's chief temptations was to worship the pagan nature gods of Canaan, such as Baal, the supreme Canaanite deity. And in an agricultural society, what a great temptation it was! Baal was the god of rain, and the pagan rituals were designed to ensure the earth's fertility. Surrounded by this kind of worship and revelry (remember, Israel did not fully drive out the pagan nations, so the practices continued in the land), it would have been easy to succumb to the temptation of worshiping the idols in their midst. By linking the harvest celebration of Pentecost to Passover, the Israelites were to remember that the God to trust *now*, with our crops and our land and the winds and the rains, is that same God who rescued us *then* from our oppressors. The same God who inflicted plagues of judgment on the gods of Egypt ("I will smite all the gods of the Egyptians") was surely more powerful than the gods of Canaan.[6]

The Canaanite approach is the forerunner of much of the modern (and postmodern) approach to life. There was no history in Canaanite religion, and no destiny either—only the yearly cycle, then another yearly cycle, and another. Their elaborate rites did not look back to a past redemption or forward to a future with God but only to the annual cycle of rain and growth. We see this in our time, in the philosophy of living only for today, with little or no regard for history and little sense of destiny. In the modern and postmodern world, just surviving the present—whether it is urban life or the life of the farmer—is all-consuming. This generation distrusts the past and despairs of the future. How different is the viewpoint of the Christian. We know where we came from and where we are heading. Later, when we look at the New Testament, we'll see how the firstfruits idea is applied more specifically to aspects of the Christian life.

## THE BRINGING OF FIRSTFRUITS

The Old Testament describes how and where the *omer* of Pentecost was to be brought. As to the place, Exodus 34:23 tells us that "three times a year all your men are to appear before the Sovereign LORD, the God of Israel." "Before the Sovereign LORD" means in God's presence, but where is that?

Deuteronomy 16:16 is more specific: "Three times a year all your men must appear before the LORD your God at the place he will choose: at the Feast of Unleavened Bread, the Feast of Weeks and the Feast of Tabernacles. No man should appear before the LORD empty-handed." During the wilderness wanderings, God was present in the Tabernacle. Once Solomon built the Temple, Jerusalem became the place of God's choice. However, in the early days of Israel's possession of the land, things were more ambiguous; the Tabernacle, for example, did not even remain in one city. There may therefore have been several suitable places to "appear before the Sovereign LORD" in those days.

Leviticus and Numbers give us the details of the ceremony itself. Leviticus 23:17–21 says:

From wherever you live, bring two loaves made of two-tenths of an ephah of fine flour, baked with yeast, as a wave offering of firstfruits to the LORD. Present with this bread seven male lambs, each a year old and without defect, one young bull and two rams. They will be a burnt offering to the LORD, together with their grain offerings and drink offerings—an offering made by fire, an aroma pleasing to the LORD.

Then sacrifice one male goat for a sin offering and two lambs, each a year old, for a fellowship offering.

The priest is to wave the two lambs before the LORD as a wave offering, together with the bread of the first-fruits. They are a sacred offering to the LORD for the priest. On that same day you are to proclaim a sacred assembly and do no regular work. This is to be a lasting ordinance for the generations to come, wherever you live.

The elements of this ceremony, along with their significance, are on the pages following:

| Element of Ceremony | Comments | Application Today |
|---|---|---|
| Two loaves, with yeast (leavened), as a "wave offering" | The loaves were to be prepared with 1/10 of an ephah of grain. This was the firstfruits itself, offering the initial part of the crop. Leaven is usually forbidden in sacrifices, perhaps because it suggests corruption and even sin. The presence of leaven in the two loaves may be a statement that even the fruit of our labors is tainted by sin; or it may simply represent that God wanted not only the raw materials but the product prepared by human hands. This would suggest that not just our resources but even our finished products belong to God. Even after we turn a raw piece of wood into a cabinet or chair, God still ultimately owns the work of our hands. | Until our redemption (and our sanctification) is complete, even our best efforts are less than perfect and may be tainted by sin. "But if anybody does sin, we have one who speaks to the Father in our defense—Jesus Christ, the Righteous One" (1 John 2:1).<br><br>Also we should realize that not just our resources but the work of our hands belongs to God, whether our job is producing software, providing education for a child, or anything else He gives us to do. |
| A burnt offering of 7 male lambs, 1 bullock, and 2 rams | The burnt offering, though it may also symbolize complete dedication, was generally seen as a sacrifice of atonement.[7] The fact that it was offered with the firstfruits underscores that even as we offer the fruit of our labors to God, we still have sin for which we need atonement. | We can worship God by returning a portion of His blessings to us, even as we receive forgiveness of sin through Jesus. Our dedication should be a natural response to our salvation. Romans 12:1 says, "Therefore, I urge you, brothers, in view of God's mercy, to offer your bodies as living sacrifices, holy and pleasing to God—this is your spiritual act of worship." |

| Element of Ceremony | Comments | Application Today |
|---|---|---|
| Grain and drink offerings to accompany the burnt offerings | The word for grain offering (minchah) is the word for "tribute" brought to a king by a vassal. This offering represented one's relationship to God as belonging to Him, offering the firstfruit of his labor as a tribute, demonstrating dedication to the Lord. | All that we do and all that we give should be with the understanding that it has all been made possible by God, and should be done or given as a tribute to Him. I Peter 4:11 (NKJV): "If anyone speaks, let him speak as the oracles of God. If anyone ministers, let him do it as with the ability which God supplies, that in all things God may be glorified through Jesus Christ, to whom belong the glory and the dominion forever and ever. Amen." |
| One male goat for a sin offering | Sin offerings (also called purification offerings) were for unintentional sins and sins of omission[8]; their purpose was to purify God's sanctuary, His dwelling place, from the defilement of our sin. | How much more quickly should we ask God to forgive us for our unintentional sins and sins of omission, since as the apostle Paul wrote, "Do you not know that your body is the temple of the Holy Spirit who is in you, whom you have from God, and you are not your own?" I Corinthians 6:19 (NKJV). |

| Element of Ceremony | Comments | Application Today |
|---|---|---|
| Two lambs for a fellowship offering, also as a "wave offering"* | Fellowship, or peace, offerings were essentially festive meals. It signifies the fellowship we have with God once our sin is removed. | Our fellowship with God through Jesus leads to fellowship with other Christians. Acts 4:32 shows us what Christian fellowship can look like: "All the believers were one in heart and mind." |
| Sacred assembly; no work to be done | This feature of several holidays may sound like a deprivation. But the idea of "rest" in Scripture is for our enjoyment, and to draw a distinction between what is ordinary and what is set apart for God. | Christians look forward to a final rest with God, a time of complete fellowship with Him. |

*What, exactly, is a "wave offering"? It is easy to imagine the priest offering the sheaf to God with a "waving" motion. A possible problem with this interpretation is that several times in Numbers 8, the Levites themselves are to be offered as a "wave offering." It is rather difficult to imagine the priest lifting up the Levites and waving them! For that matter, it is no easy thing to wave two lambs. Some scholars believe the word for "wave" or "wave offering" is better translated as "dedicate." Nevertheless, the *Mishnah* (ancient Jewish commentary) describes the priest as waving the omer in all the directions of the compass. Regardless of the translation, the intention is to dedicate the wave offering to the Lord.

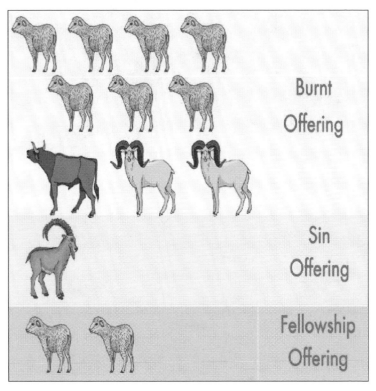

With a few differences, Numbers 28:26–31 gives much the same outline for the ceremony as does Leviticus 23:17–21 above.

## OTHER OLD TESTAMENT REFERENCES TO FIRSTFRUITS

Firstfruits are mentioned in several other verses outside of the Torah (first five books of the Old Testament—the books of Moses). Second Chronicles 31:5; Nehemiah 10:35; 12:44; and 13:31 all speak of firstfruits offerings as they recount historic episodes. The command to offer firstfruits is also found in Ezekiel 20:40 and 44:30. Each of these passages describes the literal offerings we read about in the Torah.

On the other hand, the word "firstfruits" is used differently in Psalm 78 and Psalm 105 in regard to the firstborn of the Egyptians during the Exodus:

> He struck down all the firstborn of Egypt, the firstfruits of manhood in the tents of Ham. But he brought his people out like a flock; he led them like sheep through the desert. (Psalm 78:51–52; see Psalm 105:36)

In Jeremiah, Israel is compared to the firstfruits, which were not to be consumed but were rather to be offered to God. The comparison here is that Israel was set aside as holy to the Lord, and those who "devoured" her were punished accordingly:

> "Go and proclaim in the hearing of Jerusalem: 'I remember the devotion of your youth, how as a bride you loved me and followed me through the desert, through a land not sown. Israel was holy to the LORD, the firstfruits of his harvest; all who devoured her were held guilty, and disaster overtook them,'" declares the LORD. (Jeremiah 2:2–3)

Finally, Proverbs speaks of literal firstfruits, and this is particularly instructive because it comes with a promise from God:

> Honor the LORD with your wealth, with the firstfruits of all your crops; then your barns will be filled to overflowing, and your vats will brim over with new wine. (Proverbs 3:9–10)

In return for honoring God with our material goods, God promises more abundant blessings than we can contain. This is particularly worth pondering because many Christians have come to grief over such verses, expecting God to reward Christians with wealth (the so-called "prosperity gospel") and blaming financial difficulties on their (or other people's) "lack of faith." These attitudes fail to understand what the Scripture is actually saying.

Old Testament professor Bruce Waltke rhetorically asks, "Does Proverbs promise too much? These heavenly promises of life, health, prosperity, and honor seem detached from earth's harsh realities." Is Proverbs then some ivory-tower advice, divorced from day-to-day life? Waltke continues, "Should anyone think that Solomon and other sages are dullards who cannot see or think straight, let him recall that keen observation and cogent reflection mark the sage."[9] What then do we do with such promises?

Waltke discounts one typical evangelical response, which is to say that Proverbs gives us "not promises but probabilities." The problem with this approach is that if true, it means that "the human partner is expected to keep his obligations perfectly . . . but God may keep his obligations imperfectly." This is not a satisfactory reflection on God's character.

Waltke suggests four principles to help us understand this and similar proverbs:

(1) experience does, in fact, partially validate these promises;

(2) there are "counter-proverbs" that give the other side of the picture; many proverbs (and psalms) picture the present wealth of the unrighteous, but state that God will vindicate the righteous in the end, or that it is better to be righteous with little wealth (e.g., Proverbs 16:8);

(3) much of Proverbs focuses on the future of the righteous, not on the present—whatever that present may
hold for one person or another (e.g., Proverbs 24:16);
(4) The ultimate hope of the righteous is in God's justice
and goodness in the afterlife.

Rather than reading Proverbs 3:9–10 as a flat promise
that wealth will accrue if we give our material goods to the
Lord, we do well to take it as one aspect of human experience. God's blessing generally does come to the obedient,
but whether that blessing comes via material wealth (the
how) or whether it even comes in this life (the when) is not
always given to us to know. Many faithful Christians around
the world live in poverty or under persecution. Yet one sus-
pects that as they know and trust the Lord, many of them
would count their lives as blessed, to the shame of our
Western attitudes.[10] After all, Proverbs also warns about the
dangers of wealth (e.g., Proverbs 28:11). Let us put God first
and trust Him to determine the timing and nature of His
blessings.

While firstfruits offerings are mentioned several times in
the Old Testament[11] it is not until New Testament times
that we find a detailed description of how some of these
offerings were actually made. We will therefore leave those
particulars for chapter 5.

*Counting down to a holy time
is a familiar activity for many.*

# Forty-Nine Days of Purpose?

## The Omer in Bible Times

To recap the last chapter, Pentecost is one of many firstfruits occasions in the Old Testament. The holiday speaks to us of our history and our destiny, as it helps us recall that the God who delivered us in the past is the same God we can count on for today, and for the future.

In fact, counting on God is taken quite literally in this holiday:

> From the day after the Sabbath, the day you brought the sheaf of the wave offering, count off seven full weeks. **Count off fifty days** up to the day after the seventh Sabbath, and then present an offering of new grain to the LORD. (Leviticus 23:15–16)

Following are the two primary Bible passages that determine when the counting of the *omer* begins.

> From the day after the Sabbath, the day you brought the sheaf of the wave offering, count off seven full weeks. Count off fifty days up to the day after the seventh Sabbath, and then present an offering of new grain to the LORD. (Leviticus 23:15–16)

> You shall count seven weeks for yourself; begin to count the seven weeks from the time you begin to put the sickle to the grain. (Deuteronomy 16:9 NKJV)

*Multiple Dates for Pentecost?*

One might think that the phrase "the day after the Sabbath" narrows Pentecost down to one particular date. But if we understand "Sabbath" as simply the seventh day of the week, the day of rest (which is the most natural way to understand it), we only know the day of the week, but not the week itself. By this interpretation, first you mark the day the first grain is reaped—which is not likely to be the same day for every farmer, as fields are not all ready for harvest on the same day. Then you wait for the very next Sabbath—and begin counting the next day. Thus the date of Pentecost (Shavuot) would vary for each farmer, each and every year.

*The Same Date for Everyone?*

Since the Leviticus passage follows right after the verses concerning Passover and Unleavened Bread, *Sabbath* could also refer to the *weekly Sabbath that falls during Passover* (which lasts eight days). The way the calendar functions, the Sabbath of Passover week would vary from one year to the next (though within the same general time). Therefore, Pentecost would fall on a different date each year but that date would be the same for all Israelites. The Sadducees—also known as Boethusians or Baitusim*—adopted this view.

*Enter the Pharisees*

The Pharisees, on the other hand, believed that the Sabbath mentioned in Leviticus 23:15–16 referred to the *first day of Passover*, on which there was to be a holy convocation and no "customary work." Counting from the day after the first day of Passover would put Pentecost on the identical calendar date each year.

The word for Sabbath (*shabbat*) is used 104 times in the Hebrew Bible, in reference to the weekly day of rest. A related word, *shabbaton,*§ is used four times for the weekly Sabbath, and seven times for other occasions when heavy work was forbidden. However, Scripture never uses *shabbat* to describe the special days of rest for other occasions. Therefore, it seems unlikely that the word *shabbat* (Sabbath) in Leviticus 23:15 refers to the first day of Passover.

Nevertheless, by the first century, the "first day of Passover" view had developed quite a following, and that is how the counting of the *omer* and the date of Pentecost is determined to this very day.

*An alternate name for the Sadducees, or else the Boethusians, were a subgroup of the Sadducees.

§ In modern Judaism, *shabbaton* is used for a retreat that takes place over the Sabbath.

Since the word in Hebrew for "sheaf" is *omer*, the time period between "the day after the Sabbath" and Pentecost has become known as the *omer*—and the "count-off" is known as *counting the omer*. Since the fiftieth day is Pentecost itself, it is not part of that "between" period; there are forty-nine days of "between."

The commandment to count off the days was clear enough to an Israelite in the time of Moses. But as is sometimes the case with Scripture, over time different interpretations arise. By New Testament times, the question of when to begin the counting had become a major dispute between the Pharisees and Sadducees. Each group used the same Bible passage, but with their own interpretations.

The Pharisees won. Their view became normative for the Jewish community, and that is how Pentecost (and the counting of the *omer*) has been calculated by most Jewish people for the past two thousand years and to this very day.[1] For more details concerning this controversy and how the opposing parties reached their viewpoints, see the sidebar on pages 58 and 59.

## From Earth Day to God's Word Day

Over time, Jewish people came to believe that God gave the Torah—the Law of Moses—on Mount Sinai on the Day of Pentecost. Thus, the holiday also became known as the Season of the Giving of Our Law. This traditional connection between Pentecost and the Torah is not stated in Scripture. How then did the holiday's emphasis shift from agriculture to God's Word?

One might think the traditional belief sprang up following the destruction of the Temple, as a way to keep the holiday alive and meaningful when the holiday sacrifices and rituals were no longer possible. And, perhaps the destruction of the Temple gave that tradition the full weight that it has today (more on this in chapter 4). Even so, the change seems to have begun earlier—even before New Testament times.[2]

The Bible gives no exact date for when the Law was given. It does say that the revelation on Mount Sinai occurred in the "third month," which is Sivan, the same month in which Pentecost falls: "In the third month after the Israelites left Egypt—on the very day—they came to the Desert of Sinai" (Exodus 19:1). Through an unclear process, early rabbis came to believe that the Day of Pentecost coincided exactly with the very day when God spoke to Moses on Mount Sinai. Their reasons for making this connection are shrouded in proverbial mystery.

Since the Torah was central to rabbinic Judaism, some see this as a strategic move to bring the Pentecost celebration into alignment with rabbinical ideas of what the holiday should be. One writer says, "Deep disagreements were emerging between the Sadducees of the priestly caste who focused on the sacrificial system, and the Pharisees who were more interested in prayer and study of the Torah, and who were developing the theory of the two-fold Torah: written and oral. For the Pharisees, forerunners of the Talmudic rabbis, what was crucial was their sense of a continuing unfolding tradition that was truly Torah, stemming from Mount Sinai, but not written down."[3] In other words, celebrating the anniversary of the Law at Pentecost helped to embed the Pharisees' views in the minds and hearts of the Jewish people. It ensured that the Torah, as well as the idea of the Oral Law, would be enshrined in Judaism through the yearly calendar.

In fact, the rabbis debated whether the actual day the Law was given was the sixth or the seventh of Sivan. One piece of folklore tells us that God planned to give the Law on Sivan 6, but Moses wanted the people to spend an extra day in preparation—which God evidently thought was a good idea, so He waited an extra day till Sivan 7! Folklore aside, Pentecost *actually could have been* the day on which the Law was given; we simply cannot know that it was.

In any case, the eventual shift from emphasizing the original, agricultural nature of the holiday to that of emphasizing revelation greatly influenced people's perception of the holiday. As one writer says,

> The period then became the time of ascent from political liberation to spiritual revelation—the period in which the newly free people move toward a new devotion, a new service and servitude to the God of freedom. Taken in this sense, the counting became relevant to the city-dwellers who were the Pharisees' constituency and for whom the spring harvesting may have become a distant, not highly significant process. . . . And with the waving of the *omer* and of the wheat bread gone as well, the sense of the period of the 49 days as a spiritual journey grew much stronger.[4]

In this vein, Pentecost gives greater purpose to the Exodus: God did not merely free a group of slaves; He gave them His Word and revealed what it meant to be His people (see sidebar on pages 64–65). In the words of tradition, the Jewish people were taken from a life of *avdei Pharaoh* (slaves of Pharaoh) into a new life as *avdei Adonai* (servants of the Lord).

God broke Pharaoh's hold over the Israelites in order to claim them as His own people. He then gave the Law so that they would know not only how to relate to Him but to one another. God took our Jewish people from slavery to citizenship and gave them a blueprint for behavior in this new society. Therefore, both Law and community are themes of Pentecost to this day.

Today, traditional Jews often emphasize the "journey" aspect of the *omer* period.

As the connection of the *omer* with agriculture grew more remote, the sense of the period as one of spiritual growth toward receiving Torah grew stronger. As the saying goes, "It was relatively easy to get the Jews out of slavery—but not so easy to get slavery out of the Jews." In this atmosphere, the *omer* became a time of self-scrutiny and spiritual self-improvement.[5]

As we consider these applications, some might say that we should not look to tradition (i.e., that Pentecost commemorates the giving of the Law) to speak into our lives but should only use what is in the Bible. However, we do know that Jesus and the apostles often used holiday traditions not found in the Bible in order to make a spiritual point (see appendix D). And certainly, the Day of Pentecost that Christians celebrate based on Acts chapter 1 has several parallel applications to the giving of the Law at Mount Sinai. We will explore some of those in chapter 6.

Be that as it may, some of these spiritual emphases might just as well have developed from the agricultural aspects of the holiday. For example, the above quote, which points to the necessity of the Jewish people to think of themselves as other than slaves, could just as well have developed from the blessings of the harvest motif and the attending offerings. Slaves, after all, had no crops and little to give by way of material offerings. As we were to be servants of God rather than slaves of Pharaoh, the blessings and responsibilities connected with

# THE ELECTION OF ISRAEL AND THE GIVING OF THE LAW

Perhaps you have heard or even wondered about the term *the Chosen People* as it is applied to the Jewish nation. In both the Bible and Jewish tradition, the giving of the Law is connected to the idea that God elected, or chose, the nation of Israel. Deuteronomy 10:15 says, "The LORD set his affection on your forefathers and loved them, and he **chose** you, their descendants, above all the nations, as it is today."

The election of Israel really begins in Genesis 12:1–3. There, God tells Abraham:

> Leave your country, your people and your father's household and go to the land I will show you. I will make you into a great nation and I will bless you; I will make your name great, and you will be a blessing. I will bless those who bless you, and whoever curses you I will curse; and all peoples on earth will be blessed through you.

God promised that the descendants of Abraham would not only become a great nation but also a blessing to the world. Some consider this to be the foundation of missions! Later, this promise was narrowed down to only one of Abraham's children: Isaac (Genesis 17:9, 21), and then to only one of Isaac's children, Jacob (Genesis 28:13–15; 35:11–12).

It is Jacob's descendants whom we encounter in the book of Exodus: his descendants had become slaves to Pharaoh, were redeemed by God, and then, in Exodus 19, were given the Law. Exodus 19:4–6 says, "You yourselves have seen what I did to Egypt, and how I carried you on eagles' wings and brought you to myself. Now if you obey me fully and keep my covenant, then out of all nations you will be my treasured possession. Although the whole earth is mine, you will be for me a kingdom of priests and a holy nation."

In other words, the purpose of Israel's election was to bless the nations by bringing the knowledge of God. How? By hearing and obeying the Law. Deuteronomy 4:6 says, "Observe them [the commandments] carefully, for this will show your wisdom and understanding to the nations, who will hear about all these decrees and say, 'Surely this great nation is a wise and understanding people.'"

Today, most Jewish people, though familiar with the expression "chosen people," do not understand what that means. Some look back at the persecutions and tragedies of the past two thousand years and jokingly conclude that God chose the Jews to suffer! We have lost sight of our purpose as a people.

Nevertheless, the Bible teaches that the Jewish people remain a chosen people. See Jeremiah 31:35–37 and Romans 9–11 (especially 9:4–5; 11:1–2, 28–29). God's promise to Abraham in Genesis 12:1–3 is still in effect: those who bless the Jewish people will be blessed; those who curse them will be cursed. Even in unbelief, the Jews have been a conduit of blessing to the world: through preserving the Old Testament portion of the Bible; through the lineage that God used to bring forth Messiah, Jesus; and in contemporary times, through many endeavors in the fields of education, law, medicine, and other sciences.

It is important to note that even though the Jewish people remain chosen as a nation, this is not a "chosen-ness" that guarantees personal salvation. For there is also another kind of chosenness, not national but individual.

Any person, Jewish or not, who comes to know Jesus the Messiah, is chosen. And in knowing Jesus, the ultimate purpose of being chosen becomes clear. Ephesians 1:3–4 says, "Praise be to the God and Father of our Lord Jesus Christ, who has blessed us in the heavenly realms with every spiritual blessing in Christ. For he **chose** us in him before the creation of the world to be holy and blameless in his sight."

Like Israel, Christians are also chosen to be a light to the world (see Isaiah 51:4). Because we know Jesus, the light of the world (John 8:12; 9:5), we in turn are to become a light to the world (Matthew 5:14). How? By bringing His Word, the gospel, to all people including the Jews.

the agricultural cycle might also stimulate spiritual growth. Similarly, as Christians have been redeemed from slavery to sin and are now servants of God, the blessings and responsibilities of our "crops"—i.e., whatever fruitfulness God has given to us, be it business, children, or other relationships we must tend to—should stimulate spiritual growth, and we exercise gratitude, trust, and service to God for His provision.

## Counting the Omer in Contemporary Times

Counting down to a holy time is a familiar activity for many Christians in relation to the church calendar. There are the twelve days of Christmas, and many churches mark time by such names as the Third Sunday in Advent. Many churches also count a series of Sundays leading up to Resurrection Sunday in what is known as Lent, or the Lenten Season.

Jewish people too mark certain occasions with a count. There are the eight days of Hanukkah, with each day distinguished by an additional candle lit in the menorah—and of course the weekly Sabbath is marked off every seven days. However, the most extended counting period on the Jewish calendar remains the "counting of the *omer*," which, among observant Jews, has continued since Bible times. (Today, when far fewer people are traditional than in generations past, the counting of the *omer* has fallen into disuse by many Jews.) As we saw before, Leviticus 23:15 says, "From the day after the Sabbath, the day you brought the sheaf of the wave offering, count off seven full weeks." Traditional Jews have therefore observed that commandment each year with a special evening ritual. Though *omer* literally means a sheaf, for convenience the entire seven-week period is designated as "the *omer*." It is also called the *sefirah*, meaning "counting," and the custom of counting the days is known as *sefirat ha-omer*.

The count begins on the second night of Passover and is performed each evening, which on the Jewish calendar marks the start of a new day. The person counting recites the following prayer:

> Blessed are You, O Lord our God, King of the universe, who has sanctified us with His commandments, commanding us to count the *omer*.

Then the daily count is announced: "Today is the first (or tenth, or thirty-eighth) day of the *omer*."

Most of us know what it is like to forget on occasion what day it is, be it the date or the day of the week. How much more likely are we to forget what day it is when we are counting up to forty-nine! To remember which day of the *omer* it is, many people use *omer* counters, also called *omer* calendars or *sefirah* counters. They may be mechanical devices or they may be charts. Either way, these counters are often elaborately crafted. Artistry is a hallmark of Jewish ceremonial objects, whether it is an *omer* counter for Pentecost, a Seder plate for Passover, or a special box in which to keep the *etrog* (citron) for the Feast of Tabernacles. Remember that the Tabernacle and Temple were beautifully decorated with the God-given skills of various craftsmen (see Exodus 26:1; 31:4; 35:33, 35; 1 Kings 6:18, 29). The Bible as well as Jewish tradition remind us that artistry and beauty can be an essential part of our worship.

The importance of counting during the *omer* period has led to various customs. Some people read Psalm 67 on the last day of the *omer*, because its seven verses and forty-nine words match the seven weeks and forty-nine days of the *omer* period.

Concluding the *omer* with this psalm is a way to remind us that redemption is not complete without the Word of God. Others give an amount to charity (*tzedakah*) corresponding to the count. For example, someone might give one dollar the first day, two dollars the next, up to forty-nine dollars.

As was mentioned, counting the *omer* has fallen into disuse among most Jews today. Most (though not all) who observe it are Orthodox.

## THE OMER AS A TIME TO MOURN

Many churches observe a solemn period called Lent that leads up to the joy of celebrating Christ's resurrection. Similarly, the *omer* period has become, among observant Jews, a period of mourning. This was not a biblical command but rather a later development. According to this tradition, the mourning is lifted on the 33rd day of the *omer*, a day known as Lag Ba'Omer, which also enjoys a degree of popularity among less observant Jews.

How did the *omer* period become associated with mourning? As with many Jewish traditions, more than one possible explanation has been offered, including the following:

- Mourning was a way to express the anxiousness over the growing season, when crops were vulnerable to extreme weather. But since trust in God was paramount in times of uncertainty, this explanation seems unsatisfactory.
- The custom arose after the destruction of the Temple to mourn its loss and the loss of many rituals for which the Temple was required. This seems more plausible than the previous explanation.

- The Talmud states that 24,000 students of Rabbi Akiva, the noted rabbi of the 2nd century A.D., fell victim to a deadly plague. The plague began at the start of the *omer* and was suspended on the 33rd day, Lag Ba'Omer. Jewish tradition says that the plague struck because Akiva's disciples did not honor each other sufficiently[6]—a good call for us to strive for humility.

## MOURNING CUSTOMS

The strictness of mourning customs varies according to how traditional one is. Activities such as haircuts and weddings are routinely suspended except on Lag Ba'Omer. Among stricter Jewish people, wearing new clothes or cutting one's fingernails is also prohibited. Also in the synagogue, among Ashkenazi Jews (those of Eastern European origin), *piyyutim* or poems in memory of local pogroms are read. For example, in 1096, Crusaders conducted massacres in several European Jewish communities in the weeks leading up to Pentecost. All of these prohibitions and signs of mourning, however, are lifted on Lag Ba'Omer, ostensibly because the plague was lifted from Rabbi Akiva's students that day.

## THE RELATIONSHIP
### BETWEEN JOY AND MOURNING

In Jewish tradition, joy and mourning frequently counterbalance each other. One writer explains:

As always, our Jewish religious calendar maintains a living link between ourselves and the Jews of earlier eras. The rhythms of the omer period, originating in the joys of the harvest and the associations with Passover and

Shavu'ot, were transformed into monuments to national tragedy.[7]

At the Passover seder, too, Jewish people remember with mourning God's judgment on the Egyptians even as we simultaneously rejoice over our redemption. Likewise during the seder, we dip egg into salt water to recall the destruction of the Temple alongside the joys of redemption, because "all joy must be tempered with bitterness." For the same reason, in the midst of the joyfulness of a Jewish wedding, the groom stamps on a wine glass, shattering it, as a reminder of the destruction of the Temple.

This balance of joy and sorrow is certainly rooted in the Scriptures. One could indeed make an entire Bible study of this. Ecclesiastes tells us that there is a time to mourn and a time to rejoice. The Psalms teach us to trust God in times of sorrow and times of gladness. Paul told the Philippians that he rejoiced whether he abounded or was abased; he also spoke to the Corinthians of a godly sorrow and commanded the Philippians to rejoice in the Lord always. The simultaneity of joy and mourning at many Jewish occasions reminds us that life, even as it is lived by believers, indeed holds both. For God never promised us a problem-free life but a life in which He is present both in times of joy and in times of grief.

## LAG BA'OMER

The letters of the Hebrew alphabet also stand for numbers, and if you add the numeric value of the letters in *Lag*, they total 33. So the name of this day is rather prosaic: the "Thirty-Third Day of the Omer." However, Lag Ba'Omer has become a special day because, as was mentioned, all mourning comes to a stop.[8] Because of its connection to Akiva's disciples, this day came to be known as "the scholars' festival."[9] Further, this day (which on the Hebrew calendar falls on Iyar 18) is filled with colorful customs.

Among some Jews, it is customary for three-year-old boys to receive their first haircut on this day (which is otherwise not allowed in the *omer* period), while their parents pass out wine and sweets. This is why some of the young ultra-Orthodox (Hasidic) boys may look like little girls—because their hair remains long until they are three years old!

Other Lag Ba'Omer celebrations include picnics and bonfires, at which there are cookouts. This is such a common practice in Israel that apparently, as this time approaches, building contractors there post extra night watchmen to prevent children from taking wood for their bonfires.

Children may play with toy bows and arrows, some say in remembrance of Rabbi Akiva who was said to be killed on this day while fighting the Romans. Others say Akiva defied the Romans by taking his students out to study Torah on this day—but they cleverly brought bows and arrows along to make it appear to the Romans that they were only out for a good hunt!

Many people marry on Lag Ba'Omer, or have other celebrations that are prohibited during the rest of the *omer* period.

And of course, there are various legends concerning this day. According to one, Lag Ba'Omer is the first day God gave the Israelites manna in the wilderness. The various explanations and legends can be fascinating to sort through. Is mourning lifted on this day because the plague on Akiva's students ended? Did the customs of lighting bonfires and again, bows and arrows, arise from the pagan influences of May Day, when the Swedes lit bonfires and the Germans shot arrows, all in order to chase away demons? Some might be surprised by the mention of pagan influences on Jewish culture, but the Bible gives many instances of how paganism and secularism have influenced God's people through the ages. History shows how such influences have filtered into the church even to the present day—alongside those who resist such influences. Conversely, some customs may have developed as a way to co-opt pagan practices and turn them to the service of God.

Legends aside, the lifting of mourning practices on Lag Ba'Omer can remind us that "weeping may remain for a night, but rejoicing comes in the morning" (Psalm 30:5). More specifically, we know that one day, God "will wipe every tear from their [i.e., our] eyes. There will be no more death or mourning or crying or pain" (Revelation 21:4). A plague might have been lifted on Lag Ba'Omer for the students of Rabbi Akiva; for the followers of "Rabbi Y'shua," death—the ultimate plague—will be lifted for all time.

## OTHER HOLIDAYS IN THE OMER PERIOD

Lag Ba'Omer is not the only holiday that occurs during the *omer* period. Today, several other holidays occur in this time frame; many have been instituted since Israel's establishment as a nation.

*Yom ha-Shoah* is Holocaust Remembrance Day, falling on Nisan 27, the 12th day of the *omer*. The date falls close to, but not on, the anniversary of the Warsaw Ghetto uprising. This was the largest Jewish revolt that took place during the Holocaust. Since the *omer* period is one of mourning, it is appropriate to reflect on what took place during the Holocaust. Yom ha-Shoah also serves as both a reminder and an opportunity to educate the public about the horrors that befell the Jewish people at that time, as six million Jews— one-third of the world's population of Jews—perished.

*Yom ha-Zikkaron* is a kind of Israeli Memorial Day to honor those who died fighting on behalf of Israel. It falls on Iyar 4, the 19th day of the *omer*. As Yom ha-Zikkaron ends and the next day begins, there are sudden explosions of fireworks and dancing throughout Israel!

*Yom ha-Atzma'ut*, the 20th day of the *omer*, is Israel Independence Day, on which we commemorate the 1948 establishment of the state of Israel. This is a day of public celebration throughout Israel (outside of Israel, Jewish communities often celebrate on a Sunday close to the same day). In the same way that Lag Ba'Omer provides a break in the mourning character of the *omer*, many see this as an additional day for rejoicing.

*Yom Yerushalayim*, or Jerusalem Day, on Iyar 28 (the 43rd day of the *omer*), commemorates the recapture of the old city of Jerusalem during the Six-Day War of 1967. It does not have quite the status of Yom ha-Atzma'ut, meaning not nearly as many Israelis observe Jerusalem Day as they do Independence Day.

## THE OMER AS A TIME OF ANTICIPATION

The period during which the *omer* was counted was not merely to mark time. It was a *period of anticipation*, as we awaited the fulfillment of God's promise to provide crops—if we obeyed Him. However, that anticipation had a bit of an edge to it, a bit of uneasiness, because as mentioned earlier, the weather could, apart from God's blessing, easily destroy the crops.

Note that faith and a degree of apprehension are not necessarily mutually exclusive; a person can step out in faith even as he or she faces uncertainty. In fact, to obey God despite one's feelings is often a real mark of faith. Trusting

God is not always accompanied by feelings of security. Sometimes it is a choice to do as He asks when we feel anything but secure.

It seems that God deliberately planted Israel in a difficult land, a land where, naturally speaking, agricultural success was quite uncertain. Farming it required trust in God. This uncertainty could tempt Israel to turn to Baal for success instead of to the one true God.

In some ways, our spiritual walk as believers in Jesus is no different. As we await the fulfillment of God's promises in our lives, we may experience both eager anticipation as well as apprehension (sometimes even anxiety or outright fear) over circumstances beyond our control. We are often tempted to trust someone or something other than God, and our surrounding culture offers false gods galore.

Fear isn't necessarily the opposite of courage—likewise, anxiety isn't necessarily the opposite of faith. In fact, even mature believers have times of fear or anxiety, and our faith may be strengthened when we trust God through these times. Still, He does not want us to be in a continual state of fear or anxiety. Remember what His Word says to us:

"Do not be anxious about anything, but in everything, by prayer and petition, with thanksgiving, present your requests to God" (Philippians 4:6).

"Therefore I tell you, do not worry about your life, what you will eat or drink; or about your body, what you will wear. Is not life more important than food, and the body more important than clothes? . . . But seek first his kingdom and his righteousness, and all these things will be given to you as well" (Matthew 6:25, 33).

What did a God-fearing Israelite do when the winds blew hard and it looked as though the crops might fail? We can imagine that he, too, prayed and that he sought God's righteousness, based on what God had done in the past.

An important aspect of anticipation is the understanding that we are part of a larger story with a past that teaches us to trust God for both the present and future. As Pentecost points back to how God has redeemed the children of Israel from slavery, we look to our past and see how God delivered us from sin. He led the Israelites on a journey into a land of plenty in which they were to give back the firstfruits to show their gratitude and trust for an abundant harvest that was God's to grant. As Christians, we recognize that all we have and are in this present life belong to God: "For you were bought at a price; therefore glorify God in your body and in your spirit, which are God's" (1 Corinthians 6:20 NKJV).

As the Israelites trusted God for the future based on His kept promises in the past and present as well as the hope of His future promises, so we rely on God for our future. He has promised that it will lead to the resurrection and life with Him in the ultimate "Promised Land" that He has prepared for us. This "big picture" is the basis for our greatest anticipation, and it is missing from the lives of many modern and postmodern people today.[10]

When it comes to anticipation, the traditional belief regarding the giving of the Law at Pentecost also provides much food for thought.

One piece of Jewish folklore tells us that the Jewish people were so eager to receive God's Word that they counted each day between Egypt and Mount Sinai,[11] like children who can hardly wait to receive presents. Certainly we can apply this childlike eagerness to our Christian lives, not only in our attitude toward Bible study but as we consider prayer and every other means God might use to speak to us.

Most of us have met new Christians who cannot wait to see what God has in store next. That excitement and eagerness can, and should, still be part of our lives as mature believers. Sometimes we need special days, events, or rituals, even a countdown if you will, to help us focus and regain that anticipation as we go forward in our life with God. This becomes especially true as we tend to settle ourselves as comfortably as possible, becoming forgetful of our past and future, forgetful of where we came from or that God's ultimate promises still lay ahead.

As believers who understand the "counting of the *omer*," we should be counting on God with anticipation, knowing that each passing day brings us closer to the fulfillment of His promises. We should be counting on God purposefully, asking Him to keep us faithful to those things He asks us to do—and we should count on God humbly, asking for the grace and strength to walk worthy of our calling as part of the community of redeemed people.

Much more can be said concerning anticipation from a New Testament context; you may "anticipate" this in chapter 8.

*It is quite a sight to behold . . .
streets are virtually empty except
for the sea of black hats and suits.*

*Chapter Four*

# CELEBRATING PENTECOST: CUSTOMS AND TRADITIONS FOR HOME AND SYNAGOGUE

The potpourri of Pentecost traditions described in this chapter contains lessons that every Christian should take to heart, perhaps providing a new way to old truths. Some of these customs correspond to New Testament texts or perhaps even church traditions with which you may be familiar.[1]

Most customs for celebrating Pentecost relate to the theme of God's Word. This makes sense in light of the early development of the tradition that links Pentecost to the giving of the Law at Mount Sinai. It is certainly possible that God gave the Torah seven weeks after Passover, as mentioned in chapter 3. And the Roman sacking of Jerusalem in A.D. 70 certainly contributed to the development, if not the origin, of this tradition.

With the destruction of Jerusalem and

the accompanying slaughter, the wherewithal to obey the biblical instructions regarding Pentecost was also destroyed. Later customs were not merely efforts to add a historical connection; they were attempts to replace something that had been lost. For example, the beautiful passage in Deuteronomy that describes the Pentecost worship experience—in which offering the firstfruits was so central—could no longer be enacted. In the absence of the agrarian society, the Temple, and the accompanying rituals, the focus on Torah became preeminent.

## CUSTOMS EMPHASIZING GOD'S WORD

Some customs emphasizing God's Word on Pentecost are basic and straightforward.

### SCRIPTURE READINGS

Synagogue readings for Pentecost include Exodus 19–20 (the chapters relating to the revelation at Sinai), since tradition holds that this revelation occurred on the Day of Pentecost. Within those chapters, the Ten Commandments receive special attention. People often stand to recite them, just as some church congregations stand for the reading of Scripture, particularly for readings from the Gospels.

The book of Ruth is also read, primarily because of its harvest setting. Also, Ruth's commitment to leave her old life to follow the God of Israel is seen as a parallel to Israel's commitment to follow God at Mount Sinai. Third, the book of Ruth contains the ancestry of King David who, according to tradition, was born and died on Pentecost (more about this in chapter 6). Finally, reading Ruth reminds us that *all* of God's Word is important, even the shorter or less "central" books. That's a good lesson for those who tend to skip over the lengthy and repetitive details and instructions of Leviticus, or a lesser known book such as Philemon, in order to focus on only their favorite books of the Bible.

## EXTENDED BIBLE STUDIES

In the sixteenth century, a custom developed among the Jewish mystics of Safed (a city in Israel),[2] when people would stay up all night reading and studying traditional texts from the Torah, the Prophets, the Talmud, and the Zohar, a mystical book used by Hasidic (ultra-Orthodox) Jews. Together these readings are called *Tikkun leil Shavuot*, which means "the order of service for Shavuot" (Pentecost). However, another meaning of *tikkun* is "restoration," so the phrase could also be translated as "the restoration of Shavuot."[3] The word "restoration" implies the loss of Jerusalem, the Temple, and the entire way of life on which the original and biblical celebrations were based. In following the "order of service" for Shavuot, we are also reminded that the emphasis on God's Word at Pentecost developed as a way to restore tangible ways to worship God during this holiday.

The Zohar says "the pious ones of old used not to sleep on this night, but they used to study the Torah."[4] According to Jewish folklore, Israel overslept until noon on the day of the revelation at Sinai, and had to be awakened by Moses. To make restitution for this lapse, some religious Jews now stay awake throughout the whole night. There *is* something to be said for watchfulness as we recall Jesus' sadness over His closest followers: "Then he [Jesus] returned to his disciples and found them sleeping. 'Could you men not keep watch with me for one hour?'" (Matthew 26:40). However, you may

## FIRSTFRUITS IN ISRAEL TODAY

The agricultural *bikkurim* (firstfruit) ceremonies are seeing a resurgence on the *kibbutzim* (self-sustaining collective settlements or farms) of modern Israel. Such festivals in Israel began even before the modern state was proclaimed in 1948, originating in the 1920s and 30s, and sometimes observed even outside of Israel.*

An *omer* festival based on biblical and mishnaic sources has been inaugurated [in modern Israel], symbolizing the harvesting of the first ripe grain. On the eve of the first day of Passover, kibbutz members and their children form a procession and go singing and dancing to the fields. A number of ears of grain are ceremonially cut, to be placed in the communal dining hall as part of the Passover decorations [remember, the beginning of the *omer* period is today reckoned from after the first day of Passover].

The Festival of First Fruits . . . takes place during the Feast of Weeks (Shavuot) and marks the peak of the first grain harvest and the first ripe fruits. The seven species mentioned in the Bible (wheat, barley, vines, pomegranates, olive trees, fig trees, and honey; Deut. 8:8) are represented graphically and through song and dance. There are also mass rallies to bring offerings of first fruits to the Jewish National Fund.§

* *Encyclopedia Judaica*, s.v. "Kibbutz Festivals"; also Plaut, W. Gunther,
  *Universal Jewish Encyclopedia*, s.v. "Shavuot."
§ *Encyclopedia Judaica*, s.v. "Kibbutz Festivals."

find it counterproductive to study Scripture all night long, especially if you need to go to work the following morning!

Another tradition is to stay awake a second night reading the Psalms. This ties in with the tradition that King David was born and also died on the Day of Pentecost.[5] On Shavuot, Jews in Morocco pour water over one another's heads—perhaps to help keep them awake after a sleepless night or two![6]

## PRAYER

Today Jerusalem offers a particularly poignant picture of prayer on the Day of Pentecost. Religious Jews who have spent the entire night studying the Torah make their way from their homes and synagogues down to the Western Wall, the remains of the Temple. It is quite a sight to behold: traffic stops and the streets are virtually empty except for the sea of black hats and suits, as all the religious Jewish men walk to the Western Wall. There they will rock back and forth as they *daven* (pray) recite the *Amidah* and other traditional readings from the prayer book.

## CREATIVE AND ARTISTIC CUSTOMS

Many of the Pentecost customs are artistic in nature, appealing to our senses. They reinforce not merely the facts of the holiday but the feelings it is meant to evoke. This fits with biblical accounts of art and its role in worship. From the intricate craftsmanship of the Tabernacle and its furnishings to the verbal tapestry of the Psalms, the Bible depicts our creativity as a tribute to *the* Creator who made us in His image. Creativity can greatly enhance our worship of Him.[7]

Creative customs for Pentecost include culinary arts that produce special holiday foods, decorations to adorn the Jewish homes and synagogues, as well as poetry and prose to help us enter into the spirit of the holiday. Following are some of the artful traditions.

# BREAD MAKING

Remember, God had commanded that two loaves be given as a wave offering (Leviticus 23:17). Today it is the custom (at least in Western or Ashkenazic Judaism) to bake two loaves of challah, holiday egg bread, which are said to represent either the two loaves that were offered in the Temple or the two tablets of stone on which the Ten Commandments were written.[8] Often there is a bit of artistry "baked into"—actually baked on top of—these challahs, such as a seven-runged ladder. The ladder is said to represent Moses' ascent up Mount Sinai to receive the Torah.[9]

Another interpretation of the two loaves is that they represent all of humanity: one loaf representing the people of Israel and the other representing the rest of the nations. This reminds us that God had not only Israel in view when He gave the Law, but that He intended for the entire world to benefit. God's purpose in choosing Israel was to be a light to the nations. Even so, Christians need to remember that we are saved in order to be a light to others—not attracting them to ourselves but pointing them to the source of light.

## SWEET FOODS AND DAIRY DELICACIES

The psalmist tells us that God's Word is sweet! (See Psalm 119:103.) A less obvious but often quoted reference to the sweetness of Scripture is Song of Songs 4:11, which rabbis have interpreted as Israel being the bride, and the honey and milk under her tongue as the Torah.[10]

At Pentecost we are encouraged to eat numerous holiday treats to help us appreciate God's Word. This is not a difficult tradition to embrace—most find it more pleasant than staying awake all night!

In addition to sweets, it is customary to have a number of

dairy dishes, as well as foods that combine the two. We have cheese *blintzes*—crepes that can be filled with cheese, potato, or meat (for Pentecost, we use cheese); *kreplach*[11]—three cornered dumplings that can be filled with cheese; cheese strudel; and, of course, cheesecake! Then there are various holiday cakes, including an elaborate sponge cake called the Mount Sinai Cake, *babka* (a sweet, spongy yeasted cake), and *rugelach* (a rolled Jewish pastry that can have a variety of fillings such as chocolate, cinnamon raisin, apricot, and so on). It is customary for some Sephardic Jews to eat leftover Passover matzah softened with milk and sweetened with honey to emphasize the link between Passover and Pentecost.[12] Most Middle Eastern Jews will also serve a milky rice pudding.

Several reasons are given for eating sweets and dairy products at Pentecost. First, the Bible makes twenty references to the Promised Land as "a land flowing with milk and honey," beginning in Exodus 3:8.[13] A second reason is that, according to tradition, the ancient Israelites, upon receiving the laws of *kashrut* (kosher food) at Mount Sinai, realized that their pots were unkosher—so they ate only dairy dishes that did not need to be cooked.[14] Another tradition says that Israel became so hungry waiting for Moses to come down from Mount Sinai that when he finally returned with the Law, they couldn't wait for the meat to cook! Therefore, they prepared a dairy meal instead.[15]

According to Rabbi Mendele Kotzger, we eat dairy products at this time because Israel was like a newborn child when she received the Torah.[16]

The likening of God's Word to milk is a metaphor that flows throughout the Scriptures and can be seen in the New Testament as well: "Like newborn babes, long for the pure milk of the word, that by it you may grow in respect to salvation" (1 Peter 2:2 NASB).

Another tradition suggests that those who eat meat lack restraint, and conversely eating dairy represents self-control. Is there any evidence of that? No, but it's a tradition. Those who embrace that tradition use the dairy meal at Pentecost to emphasize that the Torah teaches us to live a life of restraint and sobriety.

## DECORATING WITH FRAGRANT FOLIAGE

A third Pentecost custom in the home and synagogue is decorating with foliage, including branches of trees, flowers—particularly roses and fresh grass—which can be strewn on the floor, sometimes along with spices for the aroma. And of course this tradition aims to create an outdoorsy feeling of nature visually, along with a sweet aroma, both in the synagogue and in the home.

The most obvious explanation for this custom is that Shavuot is associated with the bringing of fruits and other crops, so there is a ready-made association with nature. While we can no longer bring baskets of the firstfruits to the Temple, we can decorate our homes and synagogues with them.

However, Jewish tradition is rarely satisfied with one explanation! Some of the numerous explanations convey spiritual lessons while others are mostly entertaining. The range of reasons for decorating with foliage includes but is not limited to the following:

- Israel found Mount Sinai blooming with greenery, so placing greenery in the synagogue recalls the giving of the Law on Mount Sinai. This is based on Exodus 34:3 as God instructed Moses, "No one is to come with you or be seen anywhere on the mountain; not even the flocks and herds may graze in front of the mountain." This implies that Mount Sinai was full of pasturage.

- According to Proverbs 3:18, wisdom, and particularly the wisdom of Torah, is *etz chaim* (a tree of life), so this connection to Torah is also emphasized through decorating with foliage.

- The sweet-smelling flowers mentioned in the Song of Songs are believed to remind us of the sweetness of God's Word, and are therefore linked with the giving of God's Law at Pentecost.

- The foliage reminds us of how Moses's mother set him in a basket of reeds so that Pharaoh's daughter could find him. According to one tradition, Moses was drawn out of the water by Pharaoh's daughter in the month of Sivan, specifically on Sivan 7, the second day of Pentecost.[17]

- God came down on Mount Sinai on the third day (Exodus 19:16), and the third day of creation was the day on which God caused trees and grass to spring forth. The connection? Both physical nourishment and God's Word are needed for life.

- Sometimes roses are used, not only to decorate the home or synagogue but also to adorn the Torah scrolls and the ark in which they are housed. The whimsical reason given is that Esther 8:14 (NKJV) reads, "And the decree was issued in Shushan." "Shushan," the name of the Persian city, sounds like "shoshanah," which is Hebrew for "rose." So . . . some believe that the Torah was given with a rose![18] But the lesson of the story is that God's Word is a sweet-smelling aroma of life.

- Israel was so afraid when God appeared on Mount Sinai that the whole nation fainted, and God used sweet spices as "smelling salts" to revive them.[19]

- When God spoke each commandment at Mount Sinai, the world was filled with sweet aromas.[20]

In all these explanations, fanciful or not, we are reminded that God's Word is a Word of life and sweetness.[21] As the psalmist says: "How sweet are your words to my taste, sweeter than honey to my mouth!" (Psalm 119:103).

Just as the plants and fruits are necessary for our physical health, we need God's Word for our spiritual health. The Scriptures compare the person who follows God's Word to a healthy, flourishing plant: "He is like a tree planted by streams of water, which yields its fruit in season and whose leaf does not wither. Whatever he does prospers" (Psalm 1:3).

Likewise, the New Testament emphasizes the importance of God's Word many times over and sums up the value of the Bible in 2 Timothy 3:16 (NKJV): "All Scripture is given by inspiration of God, and is profitable for doctrine, for reproof, for correction, for instruction in righteousness."

Similarly, God's Word is a life-giving aroma. It revives us (as in the tradition of the Israelites who fainted). In a world often marred by bitterness and corruption, it is a pleasant fragrance. As Paul says in 2 Corinthians 2:14, "But thanks be to God, who always leads us in triumphal procession in Christ and through us spreads everywhere the fragrance of the knowledge of him."

The later emphasis on Pentecost as the anniversary of God's revelation reminds us that we are redeemed *for a purpose*: to hear and obey God's Word and to be transformed to love and serve Him. "For you have been born again, not of perishable seed, but of imperishable, through the living and enduring **Word of God**" (1 Peter 1:23).

God has made us citizens of His kingdom, and we are to learn and obey His ways as we relate to Him and to others.

He has not left us clueless as to how to conduct ourselves in our new life. Not only are we born anew through the Word, but our Christian lives are thereafter to be shaped by the Word: "Blessed rather are those who hear the word of God and obey it" (Luke 11:28).

So we begin our Christian experience by being born again through the Word, and we continue in obedience to that Word, recognizing that we were redeemed to serve. The *direction* of our spiritual journey is from past to present to future; its *shape* is defined by God's Word in our lives.

## THE ART OF PAPER CUTTING

In the eighteenth century, the Vilna Gaon—a leading rabbinical figure in what would now be known as the capital of Lithuania—thought that the display of foliage was too much like Christian customs on holidays such as Palm Sunday. He accordingly called for an end to this type of decorating for Pentecost. The abolition never really caught on in a lasting or far-reaching way. However, some communities began to substitute designs of intricately cut papers, made to look like flowers and other foliage. These were called *reyzelakh*, which means "little roses."[22] At one time this practice was quite popular, but it almost became a lost art among Jews. However, the art of paper cutting has been revived in modern times and is used for many things besides Pentecost: *ketubot* (marriage contracts), for instance.

## INSTRUCTING THE CHILDREN

Pentecost is a time to introduce children to God's Word. The children begin to learn and recite the *aleph bet* (Hebrew alphabet) at age five on Pentecost. Traditional Jews bring their children to the synagogue at dawn (corresponding to Exodus 19:16, "On the morning of the third day . . .").

In days of old, each child would be put in the arms of a teacher, to reflect Hosea 11:3: "It was I who taught Ephraim to walk, taking them by the arms." Then seated on the teacher's lap, he would repeat the letters of the Hebrew alphabet written on a tablet coated with honey. After reciting the alphabet, the child proceeded to lick off the honey. This custom emphasizes to the child that the *aleph bet* is not just the alphabet; it is the letters that go into the Torah.[23] In fact, it is traditional for Jewish children to begin with Leviticus when learning the Bible—an interesting custom, considering this is one of the last books of the Bible with which some Christians familiarize themselves.

This emphasis on acquainting young children with the Word of God comes from Scriptures such as Deuteronomy 6:6–7: "These commandments that I give you today are to be upon your hearts. Impress them on your children. Talk about them when you sit at home and when you walk along the road, when you lie down and when you get up" (see also Exodus 12:26–27; Deuteronomy 4:9–10; 11:19[24]).

We know that Jesus Himself was brought up in the knowledge of the Scriptures. Luke 2 describes Jesus as "filled with wisdom," a wisdom that He displayed even at twelve years of age in His conversations with teachers in the Temple.

As Christians, we need to remember how important it is to impress our children with the Word of God. It is important to raise up the next generations to appreciate and understand the Bible—so that they can come to know God for themselves. We saw this theme underscored in the Old Testament. The New Testament also shows Jesus blessing children and welcoming them in scenes that many artists have sought to portray. A less visual but very strong example of training children in the knowledge of God's Word can be found in Timothy. By way of encouragement, Paul writes to Timothy, "I have been reminded of your sincere faith, which first lived in your grandmother Lois and in your mother Eunice and, I am persuaded, now lives in you also" (2 Timothy 1:5)—and then Paul proceeds to encourage Timothy to exercise his spiritual gifts and assume a position of leadership.

So we see a variety of Pentecost traditions emphasizing the significance, the pleasure, and the joy of knowing God's Word.

## CUSTOMS EMPHASIZING OUR RESPONSE

While most of the above traditions focus on what *God* has done, there are a few customs that emphasize our end of the relationship with God.

### THE KETUBAH (JEWISH MARRIAGE CONTRACT)

Sephardic Jews (of Mediterranean and Middle Eastern descent) practice an interesting Pentecost custom in their synagogues. They recite a *ketubah* between God and Israel. This idea is based on Hosea 2:19–20:[25] "I will betroth you to me forever; I will betroth you in righteousness and justice, in love and compassion. I will betroth you in faithfulness, and you will acknowledge the LORD." Mount Sinai is pictured as a wedding. In fact one of the meanings of the Jewish wedding canopy, or *chuppah*, is that it symbolizes the canopy of clouds that covered Mount Sinai (Exodus 19:9, 16; 20:21).

While the "marriage" between God and Israel came at God's initiative, it was up to us to respond and say yes. Israel knew this at the outset:

The people all responded together, "We will do everything the LORD has said." So Moses brought their answer back to the LORD. (Exodus 19:8)

When Moses went and told the people all the LORD's words and laws, they responded with one voice, "Everything the LORD has said we will do." (Exodus 24:3; see also Exodus 24:7)

## CONFIRMATION

The theme of responding to God's Word in obedience is also seen in Reform Temples[26] (and some Conservative synagogues) in a confirmation ceremony for Jewish teens. Many Christians are familiar with the ceremony of bar mitzvah at age thirteen for boys and bat mitzvah at age twelve for girls. Confirmation ceremonies originated in Germany in the early nineteenth century as a replacement for the bar mitzvah. The idea was that while the bar mitzvah was supposed to be the time when a boy "became a man" and could observe all the commandments, older children were better equipped to commit themselves to Judaism. The age for confirmation is generally around sixteen, though sometimes it is held later as a high school graduation ceremony.

However, the bar mitzvah was not to be so easily replaced; rather, it continues to occupy an important place in the contemporary Jewish life cycle. Many discontinue their religious education following their bar or bat mitzvah. However, for some who continue to learn more about Judaism, confirmation serves as an additional rite of passage that functions almost as a graduation ceremony. The students often write the liturgy for their own ceremonies. It has become popular to schedule these confirmations for Pentecost. The addition of this ceremony has helped to reinvigorate interest in celebrating Pentecost, particularly among Reform Jews.

Reform Judaism borrowed the idea of confirmation from Christian churches (as with other aspects of worship, such as the use of organs in the worship service). If the Vilna Gaon were alive today, he might well call for the abolition of Jewish confirmations! Nevertheless, those Jews who practice confirmation are taught that it is not enough to *know* God's Word, not enough to just *hear* it—we need to *respond* to God's Word. Through the confirmation ceremony, the students' response to God is officially acknowledged and celebrated. It is interesting to note that Christians who hold confirmation ceremonies for their children often do so on Pentecost Sunday.

## CUSTOMS THAT LOOK TO THE FUTURE

The customs described so far look to the past, the present, and the future: God revealed His Word to us (past); as we live according to that Word, we enjoy the sweet taste and aroma and help to impart it to a world in need (present); and we teach what we have learned about God to our children and future generations (future).

The future, however, encompasses not only the next generation or two but our ultimate destiny in a new heaven and new earth. While the majority of Jewish people do not focus on "end times," some Pentecost customs have a distinctly Messianic focus.

For example, people in Ashkenazic (Eastern European) synagogues recite a poem called *Akdamut*. Dating from about the eleventh century, this poem was written by Rabbi Meir during the time of the Crusades, a period of intense persecution for many Jewish communities. The poem praises God and speaks of the Messianic future. Undoubtedly it was written to strengthen the faith of Jewish people as they suffered through these terrible times. The poem is all the more poignant when we realize that Rabbi Meir lost his own wife and son in the First Crusade.

Like many of the Psalms, *Akdamut* is beautifully constructed. It includes an acrostic, whereby every two verses begin with a succeeding letter of the Hebrew alphabet.[27] Each line ends with the syllable "ta," which combines the first and last letters of the alphabet. In Jewish tradition, that can represent the reading of the Torah each year from beginning to end. When Christians consider that Jesus is Himself called the Word of God, we are reminded of another beginning and end: "I am the Alpha and the Omega, the First and the Last, the Beginning and the End" (Revelation 22:13).

Jewish tradition has often pictured the end of the world with a battle between the monsters Leviathan and Behemoth, following which the righteous will feast on them. This was meant to symbolize God's vanquishing the powers of evil. *Akdamut* ends with a picture of this ultimate victory:

> The sport with the Leviathan and the ox of lofty
> mountains—
> When they will interlock with one another and
> engage in combat,
> With his horns the Behemoth will gore with strength,
> The fish will leap to meet him with his fins, with power.
> Their Creator will approach them with His mighty
> sword.
> A banquet for the righteous will He prepare, and feast.
> They will sit around tables of precious stones and gems,
> Before them will be flowing rivers of balsam.

They will delight and drink their fill from overflowing
goblets . . .[28]

The mention of the precious stones and rivers here
reminds us of the book of Revelation as it describes the new
heavens and new earth: "The foundations of the city walls
were decorated with every kind of precious stone"
(Revelation 21:19). And, "Then the angel showed me the
river of the water of life, as clear as crystal, flowing from the
throne of God and of the Lamb down the middle of the great
street of the city. On each side of the river stood the tree of
life, bearing twelve crops of fruit, yielding its fruit every
month. And the leaves of the tree are for the healing of the
nations" (Revelation 22:1–2).

The book of Revelation, in fact, ties together the images
of greenery and fruitfulness with the consummation of our
redemption in Christ. For in the new heavens and new
earth, we find the Tree of Life from the Garden of Eden! The
fruitfulness of the land of Israel and all the many firstfruits
ceremonies not only picture God's present goodness but
point forward to the fruitfulness of the renewed heavens and
earth! Hallelujah![29]

Perhaps *Akdamut* is not a hymn you would normally
recite. But have you got a favorite hymn that you like to sing
in times of trouble, disappointment, or danger, even as
Rabbi Meir composed *Akdamut* under circumstances of personal and communal loss? Perhaps you know the story of the
hymn "It Is Well with My Soul." It was written by a nineteenth century businessman, Horatio Spafford. The Chicago
Fire of 1871 brought about his financial ruin. His only son
had recently died. Planning a much-needed vacation, Spafford
arranged to go to England with his wife and four daughters.
They sailed ahead of him on another ship, so that he could

finish up some last-minute business details. Tragically, their ship went down and the Spaffords' four daughters were drowned. Among his family, only his wife survived.[30]

How amazing, then, that Spafford could pen words like:

> When peace like a river, attendeth my way;
>> When sorrows like sea billows roll;
> Whatever my lot, thou hast taught me to say,
>> It is well, it is well with my soul.

The hymn ends by looking ahead to the final redemption in Christ—a time when Spafford would be reunited with his family. We too should be looking for the consummation of God's ultimate promises. Customs and traditions can be great reminders for us to do just that.

Eleazar Kalir is one of the best known poets of Jewish tradition. He penned the following poem for Pentecost:

Loud rang the voice of God, and lightening spears
Pierced all the heavens; thunder shook the spheres.
And flames leaped forth; and all the angels blew
Their trumpets, and the earth was riven through.
Then all the peoples writhed, aghast and pale,
Like as a woman in her birth travail.
And lo, the mountains leaped and looked askance
On little Sinai, and began to dance,
Certain each one that it would be the place
Which God would choose to hallow and to grace.
Like calves did Lebanon and Siryon leap,
Bashan and Carmel like as frisking sheep;
Tabor, too, and each high hill; but He
Who dwells on high to all eternity
Looked not on them but on the humble mound,
And while that shame did all those hills confound
To little Sinai bent the skies and came,
And crowned it with His mist and cloud; and flame
Of angels wreathed it. Then, amid the sound
Of thunder, under them that clustered round
Its foot gave forth His mighty voice; and they
Replied: O Lord, we hear and will obey,
And when they stood waiting, came the word,
That word that splits the rocks: I AM THE LORD.[31]

ELEAZAR KALIR

*The villagers responded immediately and began flocking to meet Jesus.*

# Chapter Five

# PENTECOST IN THE GOSPELS

Say you just finished making a speech and someone tells you, "You hit that one out of the park!" You don't have to love baseball to know that person has complimented you. Familiarity with the game is all it takes to understand the analogy. Similarly, we know that if someone "struck out," they failed. In all likelihood, that failure was not literally connected to baseball. Yet a degree of familiarity with the game is common in American culture, and that familiarity fills certain phrases with meaning, even in nonathletic contexts.

Similarly, numerous references to Pentecost are woven throughout the New Testament Scriptures. The harvest motif would naturally bring either the Feast of Pentecost or the Feast of Tabernacles to the minds of the contemporary audience. Pentecost was a double grain harvest (coming at the end of the barley and the beginning of the wheat harvest), so mentions of grain might more clearly point to Pentecost while allusions to certain fruits would be more closely associated with the Feast of Tabernacles.

Those who shared the culture of New Testament times and places understood allusions to Pentecost, even if the festival was not specifically mentioned.

The Feast of Pentecost, like the Feast of Tabernacles, had become filled with festive fanfare. The *Mishnah* provides a detailed description of how Jewish people celebrated first-fruits in the days of the Second Temple, which is the time period corresponding to the New Testament:[1]

> Those who lived near brought fresh figs and grapes, but those from a distance brought dried figs and raisins. An ox [this ox was later used for the fellowship or peace offering required on this holiday] with horns bedecked with gold and with an olive-crown on its head led the way. The flute was played before them until they were nigh to Jerusalem; and when they arrived close to Jerusalem they sent messengers in advance, and ornamentally arrayed their *bikkurim* [firstfruits]. The governors and chiefs and treasurers . . . went out to meet them. According to the rank of the entrants used they to go forth. All the skilled artisans of Jerusalem would stand up before them and greet them, "Brethren, men of such and such a place, we are delighted to welcome you."
>
> The flute was playing before them till they reached the Temple Mount; and when they reached the Temple Mount even King Agrippa would take the basket and place it on his shoulder and walk as far as the Temple court. At the approach to the court, the Levites would sing the song: "I will extol Thee, O LORD, for Thou hast

raised me up, and hast not suffered mine enemies to rejoice over me." . . .

While the basket was yet on his shoulder he would recite from "I profess this day unto the Lord thy God," until the completion of the passage [that is, Deuteronomy 26:3–10]. . . . He would then deposit the basket by the side of the altar, prostrate himself, and depart. . . .

The rich brought their bikkurim in baskets overlaid with silver or gold, whilst the poor used wicker-baskets of peeled willow-branches, and they used to give both the baskets and the bikkurim to the priest.[2]

So though the holiday lasted but one day, it was a national event with elaborate rituals well known throughout the land.

The Feast of Pentecost is not specifically mentioned in the Gospels. Yet when we imagine ourselves as part of the society in which Jesus spoke, we realize that some of His forty or more harvest references must have alluded to Pentecost. We can hardly think He would have neglected this feast while the other pilgrimage holidays (Passover and Tabernacles) are directly mentioned. His allusions to the grain harvest most likely pointed to Pentecost, while allusions to certain fruits might be more closely associated with the Feast of Tabernacles. These harvest references, when understood in their proper context, are rich with meaning because of their connection to the holidays.

Three notable concepts arise from these indirect references to the Feast of Pentecost: God's love, God's judgment, and God's timing.

# GOD'S LOVE

Then He said to them, "The harvest truly is great, but the laborers are few; therefore pray the Lord of the harvest to send out laborers into His harvest." (Luke 10:2 NKJV)

God loves His lost creation. He expresses that love by providing for physical needs through crops that can be harvested to feed the multitudes. His love is further expressed through the promise of a personal relationship. People who are lost can be found; those who are separated can be gathered to Him and brought into His presence. Scripture compares that people-gathering process to a harvest as Jesus speaks about His kingdom.

Remember that the Feast of Pentecost is also connected to the giving of the Law on Mount Sinai as well as the relationship between Israel and the nations. God did not give the Law to Israel as an act of divine discrimination against the rest of the world. According to Jewish tradition, God divided the world into seventy different nations (see Genesis 10). This well-known tradition says that when the seventy elders of Israel stood on Mount Sinai, they represented not only Israel but also the seventy nations of world. God purposed to bring His Word to all peoples. He told Abraham, "In you all the families of the earth shall be blessed" (Genesis 12:3 NKJV). We can see a partial fulfillment of this promise in the way Y'shua (Jesus) described God's harvest in Luke 10.

The number 70 has great significance in the Bible. Seventy descendants of Jacob came up to Egypt during the famine. Seventy members comprised the Sanhedrin, the Jewish ruling authority. According to tradition, seventy rabbis translated the Septuagint (Greek translation of the Old Testament). Remember that Jesus' reference to sending forth laborers into the harvest is in the context of His sending out seventy disciples, two by two, to preach the Kingdom of God (Luke 10:1–16).

When we see the harvest as a metaphor for God's desire to gather people to Himself, to gather them into His kingdom, we can also see the harvest as a logical expression of His love. This is important when we think of Pentecost as it relates to evangelism and missions. As we busy ourselves with the task of gathering in souls for a spiritual harvest, it is imperative that we remember God's love for those souls. Evangelism is a labor of our love, both for God and for those He is longing to save. These souls are to be handled with care, not roughly or with neglect.

While Jesus originally instructed the seventy to harvest only among the lost sheep of the house of Israel, the number 70 is a foreshadowing of God's intention that the harvest would not be limited to Israel but would gather in people from all over the world. God's love extends to every tribe and every nation.

## GOD'S JUDGMENT

The parable of the wheat and weeds, found in Matthew 13:24–30, provides insight into God's judgment through another indirect reference to Pentecost. The story ends with the farmer instructing his servants on what to do with the weeds that were growing up alongside the good wheat:

"Let both grow together until the harvest. At that time I will tell the harvesters: First collect the weeds and tie them in bundles to be burned; then gather the wheat and bring it into my barn" (verse 30).

This parable follows directly after the well-known parable of the sower (Matthew 13:3–23), in which the Word of

God is planted on four different surfaces, representing various ways people can respond to His Word. Perhaps this is a reference to Pentecost, with its emphasis on God's Word, but the following parable, with its mention of the wheat harvest, strongly suggests a Pentecost connection.

The challenge to the harvesters is that someone has sown weeds into the midst of the wheat. The owner instructs the workers to let the weeds remain until harvesttime. Why? If they seek to remove them before the crops are ready to harvest, they are likely to uproot some of the wheat prematurely.

The wheat and weeds both represent people. Jesus explained the parable to His disciples: The enemy who sows the weeds is the Devil. The harvest is the end of the age and the harvesters are angels. It is an unusual parable and we do well to avoid putting too fine a point on every aspect of it—but clearly we see God's love in that He does not want His own people harmed by the uprooting of the imposters. So in the Pentecost/harvest motif, we see not only God's love but also His judgment.

God is the judge of all the earth (Genesis 18:25). Jewish tradition tells us that God's gift of the Torah at Mount Sinai was also an act of judgment for Israel and the nations, since the Torah is the standard by which He will judge the whole world. This ties Pentecost to the theme of judgment, since this festival celebrates the giving of the Law. God in His mercy postpones His judgment. The weeds grow together with the wheat but the time will come when there is a harvest—not only to gather people to God but also to separate people out for His judgment.

Most of us don't like to think or talk about judgment. It is painful to contemplate people being separated from God eternally. That is why the harvest metaphor in this parable is so helpful. It is not difficult to see the need to separate wheat from weeds in the physical realm. Try making a loaf of bread with weeds mixed into the wheat flour. The result is likely to be inedible. The spiritual implications are clear. God's judgment is not capricious. It is not merely a punitive response to disobedience. It is a matter of responding appropriately to how people choose to align themselves, with whom they have identified, what their lives have become, all of which results from where they have "sown their affections." As clearly as weeds should not be mixed with wheat when the harvest comes, so we must see that those who have rejected God cannot in the end be joined with Him or with those who are truly, by His grace, His people.

## GOD'S TIMING

Another unusual Scripture passage, indirectly connected to Pentecost, sheds light on this subject. It is the strange story of Jesus cursing the fig tree in Matthew 21.

Jesus saw the tree from afar; He saw its leaves but when He approached it, there was no fruit. He cursed the fig tree and the following day the disciples found the fig tree had withered.

Remember that figs were one of the seven species harvested along with the wheat at Pentecost (chapter 2). But Jesus cursed the fig tree for lack of fruit, even though it was not yet Passover. Was Jesus out of touch with the harvesttimes? Was He so hungry and angry that the tree had no fruit that He engaged in what could only be described as intemperate and mean behavior? No and certainly not!

Some believe the problem was false appearances. They reason that if the leaves were on the tree, there should have been fruit as well. However, even if the fruit had appeared so early in the season, under normal circumstances it would not have been ripe and edible until months later at Pentecost.

So what is the point? Jesus was not angry at the tree. The context of the narrative is instructive. Jesus had just returned from His visit to the Temple on the heels of the "triumphal entry." During His confrontation with Jewish leaders who were plotting against His life, He pronounced God's judgment on their unbelief. By causing the fig tree to wither, Jesus illustrated His point and made a further allusion to God's coming judgment on the leadership. The common people had greeted Jesus with love and adoration as He entered Jerusalem. Yet the leaders who appeared so holy, so full of spiritual life and fruitfulness, in reality were barren and worthless, just like that fig tree. That which was barren was about to wither away as a result of God's judgment. This is a warning to all of us. It is not enough to say the right things, to appear spiritual, yet bear no fruit. We are told, "By their fruit you will recognize them" (Matthew 7:16). Even so, the presence or absence of fruit says something about our true spiritual life or lack of it.[3]

Timing is an important factor for the harvest, and the fact that Jesus expected figs when the season of figs had not yet come reminds us that God's timing is not the same as ours. He is sovereign. He determines how things grow and when the fruit will come. In the natural realm we can usually anticipate these things, but the Kingdom of God is not always predictable.

"And He said, 'The kingdom of God is as if a man should scatter seed on the ground, and should sleep by night and rise by day, and the seed should sprout and grow, he himself does not know how. For the earth yields crops by itself: first the blade, then the head, after that the full grain in the head. But when the grain ripens, immediately he puts in the sickle, because the harvest has come'" (Mark 4:26–29 NKJV).

Here the Kingdom of God is compared to the harvest inasmuch as it requires sowing and reaping, but what happens in between is somewhat of a mystery. Only God really knows what goes on while we sleep. As the apostle Paul later says, "So then neither he who plants is anything, nor he who waters, but God who gives the increase" (1 Corinthians 3:7 NKJV).

John's gospel provides another allusion to this principle in the story of Jesus and the Samaritans. Once again, the Gospels compare the harvest to people gathering, but in this instance it concerns a people among whom no harvest was expected. John 4:9 informs us, "Jews do not associate with Samaritans." Yet Pentecost is about a harvest of souls that surprises and confounds human expectations.

After Jesus' unlikely encounter with the woman at the well described in John 4, His disciples return from their grocery shopping only to find that Jesus doesn't want their food. His food, He points out, is to do God's will. Then He says something completely unexpected, something wonderful, something about God's timing and His amazing love for the most unlikely people: "Do you not say, 'There are still four months and then comes the harvest'? Behold, I say to you, lift up your eyes and look at the fields, for they are already white for harvest" (John 4:35 NKJV).

There were two seasons of planting in Israel at that time: an early and a late planting. The later planting corresponds with this reference that comes at Pentecost.

Jesus' statement reveals that things are not always what they seem when it comes to God's timing and the harvest, especially with regard to people. As Jesus was talking with His disciples, the Samaritan woman had returned to her village with an invitation: "Come, see a Man who told me all things that I ever did. Could this be the Christ?" (verse 29 NKJV).

The villagers responded immediately and began flocking to meet Jesus. When He told the disciples to lift up their eyes on the fields, the people from that Samaritan village were probably already walking through those fields in their white tunics, so that it appeared white as well. What a picture of Pentecost and the coming harvest that was about to confound and surprise—a harvest set according to God's timetable and no one else's, a harvest that went beyond the people of Israel to other peoples whom God loves. God is still reaching out to the most surprising people to this very day. We live in a time of anticipating His work in bringing the harvest, not according to our expectations but according to His purposes.

Remember that Pentecost is all about living in anticipation of a harvest that is yet to come. Y'shua shocked His disciples with a harvest of Samaritan souls. His modern-day disciples need to allow for a surprise as well. Some in the church seem to believe that Jewish people either can't, won't, or don't need to respond to the gospel. Some even teach that God is through with the Jewish people, or that attempting to share the gospel with them is not a fruitful endeavor, since the Bible tells us a veil lies over the hearts of Jewish people (2 Corinthians 3:15).

One well-known pastor commented rather coldly on this veil, saying, "I'd rather fish where the fish are biting." In effect, he questioned the value of bringing the gospel to Jewish people and even implied it was a poor use of Christian resources. But God has promised us a great harvest and His timing is not ours. It is true that relatively few Jews believe, but there are far more Jewish believers in Jesus today than there were thirty or forty years ago. If the church would do as Jesus told His disciples and lift up their eyes, people would see that the fields are indeed white for harvest. What is more, the Bible promises a greater harvest to come when the veil will be lifted and the "hardness in part" will come to an end.

The principle of the *omer*, that time of anticipating the harvest, applies here. The counting of the *omer* is not just about days; it is also about people. In Luke 6:1 (NKJV) we read, "Now it happened on the second Sabbath after the first that He went through the grainfields. And His disciples plucked the heads of grain and ate them, rubbing them in their hands."

If you will recall the details concerning the counting of the *omer* from chapter 3 of this book, we may in fact have a description in Luke 6 of what took place during that antici-patory *omer* period. Verse 1 reads in some translations, "the second Sabbath after the first," while others read, "a sab-bath." Not all the ancient manuscripts agree. But if we accept that "the second sabbath after the first" is the correct reading, then it may well refer to the second Sabbath after Passover.[4] If so, then here we find the disciples, during the sefirat ha-omer, taking barley and rubbing it together to make food for themselves on the Sabbath. The Pharisees were quite angry because they felt the disciples were profaning the Sabbath. Jesus rejected their accusations in a rather surprising manner. Referring them to the priests who worked in the Temple on the Sabbath, He drove home His point (Matthew 12:6): "I tell you that one greater than the temple is here."

In other words, the Pharisees didn't understand God's timing. They were out of touch. They were not living in anticipation of the wonderful thing God might give or do in their midst. Anticipation looks forward to what will happen; it does not exert itself to keep things as they are.

We too can be in danger of losing sight of what God wants to do in our day. When we lose our sense of anticipation, when we don't recognize the fields white with harvest, when we don't see people around us who need the Lord and don't feel a need to help harvest, we can become like those Pharisees. They were so concerned about the Sabbath that they didn't see the Lord of the Sabbath standing right in front of them. God cares about people. He is intent on bringing about a great harvest of souls and we get to help gather people into His kingdom. Let's live in anticipation of what God has promised us He will do.

What could such a noise mean
on a sunny Jerusalem day?

# Chapter Six

# THE DAY PENTECOST WAS FULFILLED

Imagine you are camped outside a tiny village near the city of Jerusalem. It is early morning. The sun is just beginning to rise. As you lie on your mat beneath the open sky, you hear the sounds of people beginning to stir in the nearby village. The pleasant hum of a new day is all around you when suddenly a strong voice breaks the calm, calling out, "Arise! Let us go up to Zion, to the Lord our God!"

It is the morning of Shavuot, the Day of Pentecost, and you have traveled a far distance from the Isle of Crete and have come to fulfill the Lord's command (Deuteronomy 16:16). The voice is that of a Temple official who comes from Jerusalem to beckon your group to complete the pilgrim journey.

Now you listen as the slow, strong moan of the shofars—the rams' horns—call to you from the parapet of the Temple. It is time to make your way up to Jerusalem, to offer your basket of firstfruits before the Lord in His holy Temple.

You still have quite a bit of a climb to get across the Kidron valley and up to the gates of that massive Temple. You arrive, having worked up a bit of a sweat, a little before nine in the morning. You are part of a throng of pilgrims who have practically reached the Temple entrance when another powerful sound such as you've never heard before stops you in your tracks.

"Suddenly a sound like the blowing of a violent wind . . ." (Acts 2:2).

What could such a noise mean on a sunny Jerusalem day? Sudden winds may come to Crete, but what could this be? You are not the only person wondering. You find yourself swept along by the press of the crowd, away from your original destination, yet not far from the Temple.

When you reach the source of this compelling sound, there is no explanation, only more questions and confusion:

"When they heard this sound, a crowd came together in bewilderment, because each one heard them speaking in his own language" (verse 6).

From the midst of a cacophony of languages you do not understand, you hear familiar words speaking praise to God in the language of your own hometown. You scan the crowd and find the man who is speaking your language, but he is surely not from Crete! How can this be? What does it all mean?

Someone next to you yells out his answer to those very questions:

"They have had too much wine" (verse 13). Several more yell out similar accusations but this makes no sense to you.

Suddenly a swarthy young man with piercing eyes, a compelling countenance, and a confident, almost glowing appearance stands up and begins to explain:

"Men of Judea and all who dwell in Jerusalem, let this be known to you, and heed my words. For these are not drunk, as you suppose, since it is only the third hour of the day. But this is what was spoken by the prophet Joel" (verses 14–16 NKJV).

And so that day, the Feast of Pentecost was fulfilled as God empowered His people to follow their destiny to bless all the nations of the world. And this was the historic day on which the power of God began to undo an ancient tragedy— the day God "reversed the curse" of Babel.

Many Christian discussions of Pentecost have been dominated by controversy surrounding the signs that marked that day. Those miraculous signs were important, not only because they were powerful but because they pointed to the great new reality that God had ushered in, a reality that we can only begin to grasp when we understand the background of the Feast of Pentecost.

As Jewish believers in Jesus, we admit to being somewhat mystified by the controversy over the signs of Pentecost. Perhaps it is the result of misunderstanding, misinformation, or biblical nearsightedness. When we only see what is right in front of us without understanding what came before, we miss the bigger picture. Arguing over the signs of Pentecost is like seeing an important, epic film and coming away having forgotten the plot but quibbling over the special effects.

## THOSE GREAT SPECIAL EFFECTS

Don't get us wrong. Special effects are great, and God's special effects trump those of Hollywood any day. But God created those special effects for a reason. They helped unpack a sophisticated plot that God has woven into many scenes throughout the course of sacred history. The signs at Pentecost pointed to past events to help us understand God's future plans. In particular, they point back to the giving of the Law at Mount Sinai. While a connection between Pentecost and the giving of the Law is not overtly stated in the Hebrew Scriptures, Acts 2 certainly seems to verify that traditional belief.

Let's go back to that time fifteen hundred years before the events in Acts 2 when the Law was given to Moses.

Exodus 20 says the entire nation of Israel was in mortal fear over the smoking mountain with all the thunder and trumpet sounds. Many descriptions beyond what we read in Exodus 20 have survived and shed further light on that special day in first century Jerusalem.

We are told that a sound from heaven, like that of a ram's horn or trumpet, increased in volume so that it was inescapably loud. I don't know if it is fair to compare the sound of the ram's horn to the sound "like the blowing of a violent wind." But whatever the sound was, it was startling to begin with and grew till it was practically unbearable. Have you ever been jolted in surprise by a loud noise that continued growing louder and louder? Whether it sounds like a howling wind or the pulsing crescendo from the blast of a ram's horn, you actually feel it throughout your entire body, even vibrating inside your head.

Along with the sound came a visual display that would make Fourth of July fireworks seem like a child's sparkler. Exodus 19:18 (NKJV) tells us that the Lord descended in fire on the mountain, but other Jewish sources provide additional imagery to this account. In an ancient manuscript called a *targum*, found in a library in Egypt, the following statement is made about the fire on the mountain: "The first commandment, when it left the mouth of the Holy One . . . as meteors and lightning and as torches of fire; a fiery torch to its right and a fiery torch to its left, which burst forth and flew in the air of the heavenly expanse; it proceeded to circle around the camp of Israel."[1]

Philo, a Jewish philosopher from the second century B.C., wrote, "from the midst of the fire that streamed from heaven there sounded forth to their utter amazement a voice, for the flame became articulate speech in the language familiar to the audience, and so clearly and distinctly were the words formed by it that they seemed to see rather than hear them" (*The Decalogue 45–46*).[2]

Jewish tradition amplified the Bible's description by telling us that the glory of God descended upon the heads of the Israelites as divine diadems when they received the Torah at Sinai.[3]

In another midrash on the giving of the Law, there is an emphasis that sounds very similar to this description of each hearing the Word in their own tongue:

"And all the people saw the thunderings. They saw what was visible and heard what was audible. These are the words of Rabbi Ishmael. Rabbi Akiva says: They heard and saw that which is visible. They saw the fiery word coming out from the mouth of the Almighty as it struck upon the tablets, as it is said: "The voice of the Lord hewed out flames of fire"[4] (Psalm 29:7). But how many thunderings were there and how many lightnings were there? It is simply this. They were heard by each man according to his capacity, as it is said, "The voice of the Lord was heard according to the strength"[5] (Psalm 29:4). Similarly, it says: "The voice of the Lord is with power (Psalm 29:4), not 'with His power,' but 'with power,' i.e., with the power of each individual, even pregnant women according to their strength. Thus to each person it was according to his strength."[6]

We cannot know if these descriptions are exactly accurate since they are not Scripture. They do seem to be in keeping with the biblical account in Exodus, especially when we add to it the poetic reflections of King David: "The voice of the LORD divides the flames of fire. The voice of the LORD shakes the wilderness" (Psalm 29:7–8 NKJV). Regardless of the specific details, we do know that God used the special effects at Sinai to grab the attention of the children of Israel and it became a defining moment the people have not forgotten. We also know that the descriptions and traditions mentioned above would have been known to the 120 disciples in the upper room, and familiar to those in Jerusalem that day.

Therefore, when the disciples heard the sound from heaven, it would have been natural to make the connection back to Exodus. And then divided tongues, as of fire, sat on each of them. According to Acts 1:15 we know there were at least 120 divided tongues that day— that is a lot of flame —more like a conflagration! Once again we have a reflection back to the Mount Sinai experience.

But before the disciples could assimilate the overpowering sound of rushing wind and the dazzling sight of flaming tongues, they found themselves involuntarily speaking words of a language they had never been taught and did not know. It must have seemed like a dream. Their mouths were moving, their lips and tongues were fully engaged, but what in the world were they saying? Perhaps in some wonderful way the Lord arranged for the 120 to know they were uttering praises, "the wonderful works of God" (Acts 2:11 NKJV).

Whether or not the disciples knew what they were saying, the crowd certainly did. As they came rushing to see what was happening, they were amazed that these simple Galileans had become such fine linguists. "Parthians and

Medes and Elamites, those dwelling in Mesopotamia, Judea and Cappadocia, Pontus and Asia, Phrygia and Pamphylia, Egypt and the parts of Libya adjoining Cyrene, visitors from Rome, both Jews and proselytes, Cretans and Arabs—we hear them speaking in our own tongues" (verses 9–11 NKJV).

This brings to mind the Jewish tradition that when the Law was given at Mount Sinai, each of the seventy elders had flame above his head representing the languages of the seventy nations of the world. Remember, according to tradition, when God marked out the nations in Genesis 10, He divided them into seventy separate nations. The incident that follows in Genesis 11 is the story of the Tower of Babel where the languages of those seventy nations were confused as judgment from the Lord.

The rabbis also teach that when God gave the Torah He gave it in all the seventy languages of the nations, offering it to each one, but only Israel was willing to hear and receive the Torah.[7] This is not a credible belief in my view, yet it does affirm an important truth: God does indeed intend His Word and His truth to be available for all the nations of the world. This is the very heart of the connection between the giving of the Law and the giving of the Spirit. Why did God give the Law to Israel at Mount Sinai? It was in order that all of the nations would see and hear. God's self-revelation at Sinai was to be carried to all peoples in accordance with His love for all the nations. And with this miraculous declaring of His Word in the many tongues of the nations on Pentecost in Acts 2, we see that hope beginning to be realized.

The languages that had been confused back at the Tower of Babel in order to separate the peoples and bring judgment on the pride of humanity were supernaturally broadcast by the Holy Spirit at Pentecost. People who had gathered for this festival could hear the truth of God in their own language. Why did God give the Spirit on the first Pentecost after Messiah's resurrection? It was so that His followers might be fully equipped to fulfill the Lord's final command before His ascension: "But you will receive power when the Holy Spirit comes on you; and you will be my witnesses in Jerusalem, and in all Judea and Samaria, and to the ends of the earth" (Acts 1:8). God's purpose was and is eventually to reunite His divided creation as the people of God, obeying and following Him together.

As Israel bore witness to the one true God in seeking to follow the Torah, the followers of Messiah are to bear witness to His death, burial, and resurrection to all the nations of the earth. Israel failed to live faithfully according to the commands once engraved in flame on tablets of stone. But now the flame of fire that once engraved the Word of God onto tablets of stone is available through the Holy Spirit to all who embrace the New Covenant. That covenant was established in the shed blood of Messiah Jesus (Jeremiah 31:31; Matthew 26:28).

As the apostle Paul would later write, "For what the law could not do in that it was weak through the flesh, God did by sending His own Son in the likeness of sinful flesh, on account of sin: He condemned sin in the flesh, that the righteous requirement of the law might be fulfilled in us who do not walk according to the flesh but according to the Spirit" (Romans 8:3–4 NKJV).

God has written His law on hearts of flesh so that we who live under that New Covenant can bear witness to Messiah, not only in what we say but by how we live—and not by striving to obey the outward law, and continually bringing sacrifices to atone for our failures. But rather we now bear witness through an inward reality that was never a possibility prior to the coming of the Holy Spirit. He empowers us to bear witness to His grace because of the once and for all atonement of Jesus' sacrifice.

The giving of the Law on the first Pentecost had now been fulfilled with the new Pentecost by the giving of the Spirit. All those who walk by the Spirit can fulfill the righteous requirements of the Law because we are righteous in our Messiah.

In a sense, Peter's sermon on the Day of Pentecost was the first fulfillment of Messiah's command to be His witnesses. Peter declared the death and resurrection of Jesus, he declared forgiveness of sins in His name, and he did so in the context of the Jewish people's understanding of the Day of Pentecost. His three references to David surely had in view the well-established Jewish tradition that King David was born and died on the Day of Pentecost.[3]

It all made sense; everything came together perfectly. Those 120 disciples were witnessing the beginning of the times of refreshing Peter was talking about. Perhaps they thought, If only the people who'd gathered in Jerusalem would all believe, then the Word, Y'shua, would certainly return to establish His rule and reign. And of course some three thousand received the Word and were baptized that day (Acts 2:41).

However, those 120 soon discovered that the Day of Pentecost did not mark the finish line but rather a starting point. Ever since the disciples saw the risen Jesus, they lived in anticipation of His coming kingdom. It was for that very reason that they were waiting, all together in Jerusalem, on that Pentecost morning. Y'shua had died on Passover and had risen again on the Firstfruits of the Barley Harvest. Acts 1:3 tells us that for the first forty days of the *omer*, Jesus was appearing to His disciples, instructing them, preparing them for what was to come. And He had finally instructed them to tarry in Jerusalem, to finish the countdown to Pentecost there.

As the day dawned and the disciples gathered for prayer in anticipation of the Firstfruits of the Wheat Harvest, they were obeying their Lord, still not realizing that there would be a harvest of people that day. But those three thousand souls who received the Word and were baptized that day (Acts 2:41) were indeed the firstfruits of a harvest that must continue until Messiah returns. Those of us who live in this time of harvest, who have the down payment of the Spirit, must still live with the sense of anticipation with which Jesus left His followers before that Jerusalem Pentecost.

## THE HARVEST FESTIVAL TO COME

Just as there was an outpouring of the Holy Spirit so that Jewish people heard about and believed in Jesus in a supernatural way on Pentecost, so an even greater outpouring in the future is predicted by the prophet Zechariah: "And I will pour on the house of David and on the inhabitants of Jerusalem the Spirit of grace and supplication; then they will look on Me whom they pierced. Yes, they will mourn for Him as one mourns for his only son, and grieve for Him as one grieves for a firstborn" (Zechariah 12:10 NKJV).

Yes, there will be mourning when all of Israel finally realizes who Jesus is, but after the mourning and the repentance, there will be great joy.

We know that a greater harvest is indeed coming, and all of us who know Him have a great part to play. May we fulfill our responsibility in the power of His Holy Spirit.

What a blessing for those who upheld the
Jewish people and honored God's love for them.

# Chapter Seven

# MORE REFLECTIONS ON FIRSTFRUITS FROM THE NEW TESTAMENT

The apostle Paul employed many vivid metaphors and colorful images to describe the Christian life and the course of redemptive history. He likened Christians to persevering soldiers,[1] boxers in the ring,[2] racers on the track,[3] patient farmers.[4] He described Christ's accomplishment on the cross as a full-blown Roman victory procession.[5] The church was to be seen as a complex human body made up of many specialized parts.[6] Paul even described himself as a nursing mother (!).[7]

Paul used another metaphor, that of firstfruits, as a teaching device. The Greek word for firstfruits, *aparche*,[8] is found nine times in the New Testament, and seven of those are in Paul's letters.[9] A common thread underlies the ways in which he applies the metaphor:

- The firstfruits are the *beginning* of what is to come . . .
- There is *hope* of more to follow . . .
- because God has promised, and therefore the hope is *guaranteed*.

Paul employs the firstfruits metaphor to remind us that God did something great in the *past*, that what He did then has application to our lives in the *present*, and that He promises to do something even greater in the *future*. If the key to the Old Testament promise regarding firstfruits is "When you come into the land . . .", the New Testament counterpart may well be, "then we shall see Him as He truly is. . . ."

Paul uses the image of firstfruits to refer to the resurrected Jesus, the first Christians in a particular geographical area, the Holy Spirit; and even in the context of Jewish-Gentile relationships!

## THE RESURRECTED JESUS

But Christ has indeed been raised from the dead, the first-fruits of those who have fallen asleep. For since death came through a man, the resurrection of the dead comes also through a man. For as in Adam all die, so in Christ all will be made alive. But each in his own turn: Christ, the firstfruits; then, when he comes, those who belong to him. Then the end will come, when he hands over the kingdom to God the Father after he has destroyed all dominion, authority and power. (1 Corinthians 15:20–24)

The resurrection of Jesus is a foundational Christian belief, and our source of ultimate hope. Paul unfolds that hope through the analogy of Jesus as the "firstfruits" of those who will yet be raised from the dead.

Just as the firstfruits came before the rest of the crop, so Jesus rose as the first of a greater harvest to come. And just as the firstfruits was a type of guarantee or down payment for the fuller harvest, so the resurrection of Jesus guarantees that we who have received Him will likewise be resurrected. The same God who gives life to the natural creation will give life to His people as well.

Notice too that in this passage Paul speaks of the entire sweep of history from Adam to Jesus. The Old Testament firstfruits were part of a larger story of redemption: one with a past, present, and future. As Paul applies the firstfruits image to Jesus' resurrection, we see that the resurrection is one part—albeit a climactic and critical part—of the entire story that spans the first entrance of sin into the world to the final new heavens and new earth.

This sweeping history has implications for us as *individuals* (we will be resurrected), as well as a *community* (the church will live together in the new heavens and new earth), and it also has implications for the *world*. Firstfruits in the Old Testament provided an opportunity for Israel to trust God rather than Baal and the Canaanite nature gods. God understood the temptation that the Israelites would face in the midst of Canaanite influences. Firstfruits was a reminder not only to Israel but to her neighbors that the God of Abraham, Isaac, and Jacob was the Creator and Provider, in contrast to the powerless false gods they might be tempted to follow.

The firstfruits imagery surrounding the resurrection of Jesus provides a similar reminder. As N. T. Wright points out, Jewish people in the first century understood that resurrection indicated the arrival of the Kingdom of God. Says Wright:

> The present "ordering" . . . of society places Caesar at the top, his agents in the middle, and ordinary people at the

bottom; the creator's new ordering will have himself at the top, the Messiah—and his people . . .—in the middle, and the world as a whole underneath, not however exploited and oppressed but rescued and restored, given the freedom which comes with the wise rule of the creator, his Messiah, and his image-bearing subjects. This passage thus belongs with Romans 8, Philippians 2:6–11 and 3:20–21 as, simultaneously, a classic exposition of the creator God's plans to rescue the creation, and a coded but powerful reminder to the young church, living in Caesar's world, that Jesus was lord and that at his name every knee would bow.[10]

The firstfruits of the crops and the ensuing harvest reminded Israel that God is the living God, and Baal was . . . a disposable, man-made product.

Likewise—in a far more powerful way—the firstfruits, which is the resurrection of Jesus, reminds us today that God is God, and that the rulers and powers of this world will pass on. How encouraging for all of us, and especially for those Christians living under persecution and oppression in many countries of the world. Jesus alone is Lord, and not the dictators and despots of this world. And the resurrection is the demonstration of that fact! Here's who holds the real power:

> Then the end will come, when he hands over the kingdom to God the Father after he has destroyed all dominion, authority and power. (1 Corinthians 15:24)

## THE FIRST BELIEVERS

Paul also uses firstfruits as a metaphor for those who first came to faith in Jesus in one geographical area or another.

So, for instance, in Romans 16:5 (NKJV) Paul passes along his greetings in this way:

> Greet my beloved Epaenetus, who is the **firstfruits** of Achaia to Christ.

Likewise, we have 1 Corinthians 16:15 (NKJV):

> You know the household of Stephanas, that it is the **first-fruits** of Achaia, and that they have devoted themselves to the ministry of the saints.

Whether or not Epaenetus was part of the household of Stephanas we do not know, though both are from Achaia (in southern Greece). Paul could have used "firstfruits" to refer not to the very first Christian individual but to the entire group that represented the first people in the area to receive Jesus. Once again, the mention of "firstfruits" implies a fuller harvest to come. Paul's choice of words shows that he anticipated more people to come to faith.

The timing of the spiritual harvest differs from that of the physical harvest. While the farmer had a reasonable sense of a time frame for harvesting, we have less of a sense when God might move. Earlier we mentioned that some have seen Jewish missions as wasteful because relatively few Jewish people are coming to faith in Jesus as Messiah. While there has not been a mass "people movement" among the Jewish people (perhaps ½ to 1 percent of Jewish people profess faith in Jesus), at times we do see an increase—the past few decades being one of those times.

Had those first missionaries not stepped out in faith in anticipation of a fuller "harvest," would we see as many believers in Jesus as we do today?

As was mentioned in chapter 5, Jesus told His disciples that the fields were ripe for harvest and pointed to the Samaritans, who were probably the last people the disciples would have expected to see in the harvest. It was within that context that Jesus also pointed out, "Thus the saying 'One sows and another reaps' is true. I sent you to reap what you have not worked for. Others have done the hard work, and you have reaped the benefits of their labor" (John 4:37–38).

This ought to encourage us; the first results of mission work in any area should, in faith, be seen as the beginnings of a crop. Faith, Hebrews tells us, is "being sure of what we hope for and certain of what we do not see" (Hebrews 11:1). This was true of the biblical heroes that Hebrews mentions as examples of faith; it was true also of countless unnamed Israelite farmers who, in faith, expected a full harvest before they could see it. Even so, Paul expected more people to come to faith in Christ, though they were known only to God.

May that be true of us: that we in faith anticipate God's continued working for a greater harvest of believers, and be co-laborers to that end, whether our mission field is to people overseas or in the house next door.

## THE HOLY SPIRIT

Paul also applies the firstfruits metaphor to the Holy Spirit:

Not only so, but we ourselves, who have the **firstfruits** of the Spirit, groan inwardly as we wait eagerly for our adoption as sons, the redemption of our bodies. (Romans 8:23)

Are we to understand that we have only part of the Spirit, with the rest of the Spirit to come at a future time? No, because Paul exhorts the believers at Ephesus to "be filled with the Spirit" (Ephesians 5:18). In speaking of the Holy Spirit, Paul uses the image of firstfruits in a slightly different way. His meaning becomes clearer when combined with the concept of "down payment" or "deposit" (in Greek, *arrabon*):

> Having believed [in Christ], you were marked in him with a seal, the promised Holy Spirit, who is a **deposit** guaranteeing our inheritance until the redemption of those who are God's possession—to the praise of his glory. (Ephesians 1:13–14)

What is the "inheritance" that Paul mentions? It is the fullness of redemption that God has promised us, our eternal relationship with God in a new resurrected body, and in a new heaven and new earth. The Spirit is the "firstfruits" of an even deeper, fuller relationship with God that is to come. Sometimes this is described as the "now but not yet" reality: we have begun to experience our final destiny with God, but we have not yet experienced its fullness. As author G. M. Burge observed,

> The Spirit for Paul, then, is an interim gift, a prelude and foretaste of the glory that is to come. The Spirit is not simply to comfort and strengthen believers during the trials of the world; the Spirit is also there to remind them of the future, that they possess identity as aliens in this world as they await their complete glorification . . . in Christ.[11]

Perhaps this is a helpful analogy: As Christ's transfiguration (see Matthew 17:1–2) was a foretaste of the glory to come for Peter, John, and James, so the abiding presence of the Spirit is a foretaste for us. And, while the transfiguration was momentary, the indwelling Spirit is a permanent gift of God.[12]

## THE JEWISH PEOPLE

Finally, Paul uses the firstfruits metaphor to speak of the place of the Jewish people in God's plan, and the relationship between Jewish and Gentile believers in the body of Christ:

> For if their [the Jewish people as a whole] rejection is the reconciliation of the world, what will their acceptance be but life from the dead? If the part of the dough offered as **firstfruits** is holy, then the whole batch is holy; if the root is holy, so are the branches. If some of the branches have been broken off, and you, though a wild olive shoot, have been grafted in among the others and now share in the nourishing sap from the olive root, do not boast over those branches. If you do, consider this: You do not support the root, but the root supports you. (Romans 11:15–18)

Romans 9–11 describes the place of the Jewish people within God's plan. We see the blessings that have come to the Jewish people[13] and the conundrum of how they can be God's people while the majority do not believe in Jesus.[14] Paul has talked about the remnant—the minority of Jewish people who followed God in Old Testament times as well as in New.[15] Now in Romans 11, Paul warns the Gentile Christians against pride when they see the unbelief of the Jewish people. Paul explains that the Jews have not ceased to be God's people; any "rejection" by God is not to be seen as a complete casting off—the faithful remnant still exists, and a day will come when Israel as a whole will know and follow the Lord. In the meantime, the Gentile Christians are exhorted to realize humbly that they have been grafted in as wild branches into a natural tree, and God is equally able to cut off Gentiles and restore Jews to faith. And if unbelieving Israel turns back to God in faith, they will be accepted and "grafted back in." This is Paul's hope![16]

In verses 15–18, Paul suggests that the unbelief of Israel has actually helped further the gospel among the Gentiles. He reflects that if God could use Israel's unbelief for good, when Israel turns to Jesus, even greater blessings will come.

In verse 16 Paul also sets up a parallel image.

> If the part of the dough offered as firstfruits is holy,
>     then the whole batch is holy;
> If the root is holy, so are the branches.

Here "the part of the dough offered as firstfruits" is parallel to "the root," and "the whole batch" is parallel to "the branches." Paul does not talk about the Gentiles until verse 17; "the whole batch" and "the branches" in verse 16 are speaking of the nation of Israel. But who or what is the "firstfruits" (and "root")?

Scholars tend to cluster around two opinions: either the firstfruits are the patriarchs to whom God's promises first came (Abraham, Isaac, and Jacob), or else they are the remnant of Jewish people who follow God.

The first view would state that the word "holy" means "set apart by God for a purpose." God called the patriarchs and promised to make a special nation through their descendants. Therefore as God "set aside" the patriarchs for His purposes, He set aside their descendants, the Jewish people, as a separate nation. If this is the meaning, then Paul is arguing that the Jewish people are still a chosen people in God's purposes.

The second view is that Paul meant for the firstfruits to represent the remnant of Jewish believers. The idea would be that in some way the remnant "sanctifies" the rest of the Jewish people—perhaps by acting as a channel of God's grace to the rest of the people (think of how God told Abraham that He would spare Sodom for the sake of a small number of believers, if they could be found), or again, as a kind of guarantee that more Jewish people will turn to Christ.

Many people favor the first view, that the firstfruits are the patriarchs, because:

- the use of the word "firstfruits" parallels "root" in the passage;
- the patriarchs are called a "root" in other examples of Jewish literature of the time;[17]
- Romans 11:28–29 provides a correlation to this view: "As far as the gospel is concerned, they are enemies[18] on your account; but as far as election is concerned, they are loved on account of the patriarchs, for God's gifts and his call are irrevocable."

Whether Paul is using the firstfruits metaphor to refer to the patriarchs or the Jewish remnant, either view points out that the Jewish people remain as a special people of God— even in unbelief. Church history demonstrates how Paul's warning has, at times, been ignored, with tragic results. One wonders if he foresaw the way that some in the church have attempted to relegate the Jewish people to the ash heap of history, or engaged in anti-Semitic actions. This has been a source of shame and reproach and has not helped the Jewish people to embrace faith in Jesus as Messiah. On the other hand, what a blessing it has been for those who upheld the Jewish people and have honored God's love for them.

A cautionary word for today: the fact that Jewish people remain a unique and special people with a role in God's plan does *not* mean that they do not need to hear the gospel! While Israel as a nation remains a chosen people, individual Jewish people are still lost without the atonement for sin that only comes through Jesus the Messiah. This is why Paul cries out in Romans 9:2–4 that he has "great sorrow and unceasing anguish in my heart. For I could wish that I myself were cursed and cut off from Christ for the sake of my brothers, those of my own race, the people of Israel." Paul visited the synagogue in each city he came to, such as in Corinth where "every Sabbath he reasoned in the synagogue, trying to persuade Jews and Greeks. When Silas and Timothy came from Macedonia, Paul devoted himself exclusively to preaching, testifying to the Jews that Jesus was the Christ" (Acts 18:4–5). We can be sure that Paul was not testifying that Jewish people are reconciled to God without His Messiah Jesus. In fact it was because they were God's people and *because* of the blessings and promises that Paul was especially anguished over the many who had not yet fulfilled their calling as a people of God.

## ALL BELIEVERS IN JESUS

He chose to give us birth through the word of truth, that we might be a kind of **firstfruits** of all he created. (James 1:18)

Here James uses the term "firstfruits" to describe all believers as the first element in the final redemption that will come to the entire universe. Once again we see firstfruits as the beginning of God's provision, with the promise of more to come.

The vision here goes beyond the evangelization of the world. The redeemed people of God are the first to take part in what will one day be a fully redeemed creation. Our redemption is a pledge or guarantee of God's promise to redeem the universe.

James has observed in the previous verse that "every good and perfect gift is from above, coming down from the Father of the heavenly lights, who does not change like shifting shadows" (1:17). Therefore the new birth that God has given us (verse 18) is a gift. The emphasis on ethical living throughout the book of James suggests that we, as the first-fruits of the final redemption, should be God's agents for change in the world around us. This challenges us as Christians to ask ourselves what we can be doing to extend Christ's love to the world, not only by evangelism but by helping the poor, working with AIDS orphans, helping the environment, and so forth. Regardless of one's beliefs about eschatology, God intends for Christians—as the firstfruits of a greater redemption to come—to help bring in not just a harvest of "souls" but a harvest of righteousness in society.

Followers of Christ for centuries have been so, as seen in examples such as medical missions. William Wilberforce stands as a shining example; his well-known fight to abolish the British slave trade in the nineteenth century was an outworking of his faith.

People, after all, are more than pieces of fruit or stalks of grain. A sheaf of barley has no obligations and no responsibilities; but the church as firstfruits has both. May God help us fulfill our responsibilities even as we cry out, "Maranatha, Come Lord Jesus," anticipating the fullness of His kingdom that will establish everlasting righteousness.

## PERSECUTED BELIEVERS

The final redemption is not yet complete. Until it is, we can expect trials and tribulations as we follow in the footsteps of the apostles, and of Jesus Himself. Our final look at firstfruits is from the book of Revelation, and a scene from the future:

> Then I looked, and there before me was the Lamb, standing on Mount Zion, and with him 144,000 who had his name and his Father's name written on their foreheads. And I heard a sound from heaven like the roar of rushing waters and like a loud peal of thunder. The sound I heard was like that of harpists playing their harps. And they sang a new song before the throne and before the four living creatures and the elders. No one could learn the song except the 144,000 who had been redeemed from the earth. These are those who did not defile themselves with women, for they kept themselves pure. They follow the Lamb wherever he goes. They were purchased from among men and offered as **firstfruits** to God and the Lamb. No lie was found in their mouths; they are blameless. (Revelation 14:1–5)

This passage speaks of a group known as the 144,000. This is not the place to promote one view or another regarding the specific identity of this group (many commentaries are available on the subject). However, it is clear that they are:

- believers in Jesus, and
- "offered as firstfruits" to God. Revelation 7:14 suggests that the 144,000 will be martyred because of their faith (cf. Revelation 6:9–11).

The focus of this passage is not on who these 144,000 are but rather on the reality that suffering, persecution, and even martyrdom await many of God's people. Even as the church experienced persecution at the hands of Rome in the first centuries, and is still persecuted today in many parts of the world, so it will also be in the future.

# A NOTE ON PAUL AND PENTECOST

Two passages mention Paul's travel plans in connection with Pentecost. The first is found in Acts 20:16:

> Paul had decided to sail past Ephesus to avoid spending time in the province of Asia, for he was in a hurry to reach Jerusalem, if possible, by the day of Pentecost.

This verse recounts Paul's decision to bypass Ephesus (located in the Western part of what today is Turkey; "Asia" is approximately modern Turkey). It seems he altered his plans in order to try to reach Jerusalem in time for Pentecost. The rest of Acts 20 recounts Paul's sending for the Ephesian elders, his farewell speech to them, and then in Acts 21, Paul's ensuing journey to Jerusalem. That he succeeded in arriving at or in time for Pentecost seems indicated by Acts 21:27 in which "some Jews from the province of Asia saw Paul at the temple." This would indicate that Jews from the Diaspora had come to Jerusalem, which would be expected at a pilgrimage festival like Pentecost.

*CHRIST in the Feast of Pentecost*

In what sense are such Christians firstfruits? If they die for their faith, they are considered as having offered their lives in service to God. This is a less common meaning of "firstfruits," but one that makes sense in this passage where martyrdom is considered an "offering" to God. This is not to say that God requires human sacrifice. Rather, those who lose their lives in their stand for God have given a firstfruits offering because they trusted God's promise that there was more to life than the brief sojourn of mortal men and women on this earth.

The Torah commands all Jews in Israel to make the pilgrimage, but in practice those living in the Diaspora did not always go up to Jerusalem. Those farthest away would perhaps go once in their life, and that would likely be on a Passover. While Jews living in the Diaspora were not all expected to be in Jerusalem for Shavuot, it would certainly have been considered meritorious to do so. Paul's eagerness to arrive in Jerusalem by Shavuot could just as well have been for Spirit-inspired evangelistic motives (Acts 20:22–24; compare Acts 23:11) as to observe the festival.

The second passage in which Paul mentions Pentecost is found in 1 Corinthians 16:8–9:

> But I will stay on at Ephesus until Pentecost, because a great door for effective work has opened to me, and there are many who oppose me.

In this situation, it seems possible that Paul was planning to celebrate Pentecost in the Diaspora, rather than in Jerusalem. He is planning strategically, taking into account both the opportunities for ministry as well as his opposition.

## SUMMARY

Throughout the New Testament, we see firstfruits imagery used in various ways, including Jesus' resurrection, the Holy Spirit, and believers as the beginnings of the new creation. In all cases it reminds us:

- Our redemption has begun, with the fullness yet to come. As Jesus has risen, so we will too. As we have come to Christ, more will follow. The Holy Spirit who guarantees our final redemption is the first part of our vital new relationship with God, with more to come. The existence of the church, with its obligations and responsibilities to act as the church, presages the redemption of the world.

- All that God has promised will happen. The same God who gives life to the world of nature, causing growth to spring forth, will give life to us, now and in the future. God is faithful to His Word. May we too be faithful in responding to God's gift of life and growth.

*Looking back is also a
time of looking forward.*

# Chapter Eight

# A PENTECOST MEDITATION: HOW TO ANTICIPATE CHRIST'S RETURN

Thinking back to what we've learned about the *omer* period, we see a rhythm during this time unlike any other on the Jewish calendar. Yes, there are rhythms related to other festivals, but in this particular period of time—forty-nine days—there is a count every single night. It affects the daily lives of religious Jews by "imposing" anticipation in a way that many Christians do not experience. Even the lighting of Advent candles might not have quite the same impact.

In essence, the period of anticipation, or expectancy, helps reflect a mind-set with respect to God's future purposes. We talked about anticipation for the Israelite farmer in the Old Testament. But we also find the theme of anticipation throughout the New Testament. Consider Luke 12:35–36:

Be dressed ready for service and keep your lamps burning, like men waiting for their master to return from a wedding banquet, so that when he comes and knocks they can immediately open the door for him.

Who is the master for whom we are to be waiting, for whom our lamps are to be kept burning? None other than Jesus! Many Christians have found their imaginations captivated by thoughts and speculations concerning the return of Christ. Just prior to Y'shua's ascension, His disciples asked this very question and the response did not encourage their speculation or ours. He said, "It is not for you to know times or seasons which the Father has put in His own authority" (Acts 1:7 NKJV). That phrase, "times or seasons" (*chronoi* and *kairoi* in the Greek), refers to both the duration of the period leading up to the return of Christ and to its character.[1]

The fact that Jesus Himself told us we couldn't know these things has not dampened the speculation, as many have tried to pin down a date for His return. The little book *88 Reasons Why the Rapture Could Be in 1988* no doubt underwent a radical price cut in 1989![2]

While Jesus discouraged His disciples from speculating on the exact time of His return, He did not mean that we shouldn't be longing for and living in anticipation of that event. We certainly should anticipate and count down the days until the return of Christ, which is our blessed hope (Titus 2:13). In fact, for Christians, the countdown of the *omer* can be seen as a metaphor for the countdown to the return of Jesus.

We are currently in between times—after the coming of Jesus as our sacrificial atonement and before His return. Jesus encouraged, even commanded us, to live a life filled with anticipation, of expectancy, during this time. In fact,

He not only encouraged the sense of anticipation, but He gave us, as His disciples, tangible ways to look back on His promise and forward to His return.

## COMMUNION

Communion, though understood differently by Christians of various denominations, touches a common chord in all believers. The bread and cup were given that we might own what Christ did for us at Calvary in a very personal way. Note that Communion was given in the context of a celebratory meal (Passover) where His followers had gathered to commemorate redemption from physical slavery. Today, Christians gather together and acknowledge the price that Jesus paid for our spiritual redemption from sin. The apostle Paul added a time frame to our understanding of Communion: "For whenever you eat this bread and drink this cup, you proclaim the Lord's death *until he comes*" (1 Corinthians 11:26).

Just as God commanded the children of Israel to observe various feasts and festivals to remember what He had done, Jesus commanded His disciples to celebrate this special supper to remember His death, and to remember that He is coming again. Each time we take Communion, we may consider ourselves that much closer to the day we will see Jesus face-to-face. Whereas it is important to remember what Christ did to secure our redemption, we greatly miss the point if we do not take Paul's words as an occasion to anticipate His return. Looking back is also a time of looking forward with most Jewish festivals; so it should also be with Communion.

# STEWARDSHIP

As Christ's followers, we are to oversee the people and things God has entrusted to our care as those who will answer to Him. In Luke 12:35–48, Jesus told a story to help His disciples understand the importance of anticipating His return. In this passage, Jesus emphasized just and ethical treatment of those who must look to the steward for their well-being. The steward is to anticipate the master's return and to exercise faithfulness in handling matters according to His master's will and His ways.

Part of looking forward to Christ's return is being constantly aware of how we are handling our resources, our authority, our relationships—knowing that they are not merely ours but God's. We anticipate His return by caring for all He has entrusted to us in such a way that at the moment of His return, whenever that might be, He will be pleased with how we are carrying out our responsibilities. Conversely, the person who is careless or abusive with that which the master has entrusted to him or her is not living in the hope and expectation of the Master's return.

## KEEPING HIS COMMANDMENTS

In John 13 we see that Jesus used Passover as an occasion to announce that He was going away (verse 33) and to give His disciples a new commandment to fulfill in His absence: to love one another (verses 34–35). Following the disciples' expressions of anxiety over His leaving, Jesus promised to come again to receive His disciples to Himself (John 14:3). He then spoke of what the disciples should expect to be doing while He is away: the works that Jesus has done, and even greater works, asking anything in His name (verses 12–13). Then He adjured them, "If you love Me, keep My commandments" (John 14:15 NKJV).

The obedience issue here is similar to that of stewardship with one very important addition. Obedience as a steward is a matter of appropriate behavior as a servant—doing one's duty to one's master. Here Jesus gave His disciples the Law of love for one another, adding that His commandments are not merely to be performed out of duty but that obedience to Jesus is to be the natural outcome of our love for Him. Rather than lessen our responsibility as servants, this elevates it from duty to our Master's position to loyal love for His person. When Christ returns, will He find us merely performing our functions appropriately that we might receive a commendation for our work? Or will He also find us seeking to demonstrate our love and trust by carrying out His commandments from the heart?

## ABIDING WITH THE HOLY SPIRIT

Continuing in John 14, we see Jesus' promise that the Holy Spirit would come and abide with His disciples following His departure (verse 16). This promise was given, again, to reassure the disciples who could not imagine life without their Master. He was going to leave but would not leave them as orphans (verse 18). In fact, Jesus promised to come to the disciples in a way that the world will not see (verse 19) but they would. The Father Himself would send the Holy Spirit in Christ's name (verse 26). Jesus promised that the Spirit would both teach the disciples and help them remember all that He (Jesus) had said to them. Moreover, Jesus reminded them that He would soon go to the Father but would come back to them (verse 28).

As we have seen, the Holy Spirit is the firstfruits of an

intimate relationship with God. The gospel of John sheds further light, as Jesus indicated that the Holy Spirit is, in a sense, the firstfruits of His return. The sending of the Spirit was promised in the context of Jesus "coming to" the disciples, yet it is not THE coming, which is still to be expected even after the giving of the Holy Spirit. As Jesus promised, the Father sent the Spirit (on the Day of Pentecost) in Christ's name to Christ's followers to continue teaching them and to help them remember the things Christ had told them. The Holy Spirit teaches us despite Jesus' physical absence, and reminds us of those things He said in His Word. As we open ourselves daily to the influence of the Holy Spirit, Jesus is with us in a mysterious way. The more we avail ourselves of the presence and power of the Holy Spirit, the better we will know Jesus, and the more we will long to see Him face-to-face.

## PROCLAIMING THE GOSPEL

Prior to His ascension, Jesus gave numerous commands to His disciples to go forth and proclaim the good news. The references for and nuances of these commands will be cited and more fully explored in chapter 9. This command, best known as the Great Commission, follows logically on the heels of Communion, stewardship, obeying Christ's commands, and abiding in the Holy Spirit.

Even as Communion proclaims "the Lord's death until he comes" (1 Corinthians 11:26), so does telling the gospel story to other people. When we testify to our belief in Jesus, we not only remember what He did at Calvary, but we own it in a very personal way. Each time we tell someone what the Lord did to save us—and to save them—we partake afresh of that grace, both affirming and experiencing it as we offer it to others.

The gospel has been entrusted to us, as Paul wrote to the Thessalonians: "But as we have been approved by God to be entrusted with the gospel, even so we speak, not as pleasing men, but God who tests our hearts" (1 Thessalonians 2:4 NKJV). Therefore we are to be good stewards of the gospel, which means seeing that it is offered to those who are perishing. Likewise, we see in 2 Corinthians that God has "committed to us the word of reconciliation" and that we are to be Christ's ambassadors, imploring people to be reconciled to God (2 Corinthians 5:19–20 NKJV). Once again, we see that we, as Jesus' disciples, are stewards of the word of reconciliation.

We also see how Jesus appealed to love as the motivation to proclaim the gospel. In John 21, Jesus asked Peter three times, "Do you love me?" and upon each declaration of Peter's love, Jesus instructed him, "Feed my lambs" (verse 15), "tend my sheep" (verse 16), and "feed my sheep" (verse 17). Lest we mistake this command for a pulpit position in a protected church situation, Jesus went on to predict Peter's martyrdom (verses 18–19). And in verse 23, the Lord mentioned His return. It is clear that His command to Peter was to be obeyed out of love, though Peter himself would not live to see Christ's return.

Finally, we see through various Scriptures (e.g., Romans 15:18–19; 1 Thessalonians 1:5) that gospel proclamation is effective when it is done in and through the power of the Holy Spirit. It is no coincidence that on the day of Pentecost when the Spirit was given, the disciples proclaimed God's Word in languages unknown to them. The Lord had not only provided the motivation but the means to proclaim the gospel—His own Spirit.

*If we can catch a glimpse of the bigger picture,
it will give us hope to press on.*

# THE COUNTDOWN COMMISSION

Jesus gave His disciples a number of action points with which they were to occupy themselves (and by extension, we are to occupy ourselves) until He returns. Of the points mentioned, gospel proclamation seems to be the one that many people find intimidating. Perhaps that is why our Messiah chose the *omer* period that led up to Pentecost to give this critical instruction not once but several times.

During this time, Jesus did not dwell with His disciples, but He was "seen by them during forty days and [spoke] of the things pertaining to the kingdom of God" (Acts 1:3 NKJV). In other words, Jesus chose various occasions during that time between His resurrection, the fulfillment of the first "Firstfruits," and His ascension, the fulfillment of the second "Firstfruits," to instruct His disciples.

That instruction, at least the part God chose to make public in the New Testament, focused almost exclusively on the responsibility to be witnesses, preach the gospel, and go into all the world. As much as the countdown to Pentecost was a time of preparation for the wheat harvest, so for the followers of Jesus we are to proclaim the gospel as we count down to a harvest of souls. As we commit ourselves to obedience to Messiah's instructions, we can expect to see the fields white for the harvest.

Let's look more closely at four of the major teachings about the proclamation of the gospel Jesus gave us during this special "Messianic Omer."

## THE CONTEXT OF THE MESSAGE WITHIN GOD'S PLAN FOR THE AGES

The first *omer* statement, chronologically speaking, is found in Luke 24:44–48 (NKJV):

> Then He said to them, "These are the words which I spoke to you while I was still with you, that all things must be fulfilled which were written in the **Law of Moses** and the **Prophets** and the **Psalms** concerning Me." And He opened their understanding, that they might comprehend the Scriptures. Then He said to them, "Thus it is written, and thus it was necessary for the Christ to suffer and to rise from the dead the third day, and that repentance and remission of sins should be preached in His name to all nations, beginning at Jerusalem. And you are witnesses of these things."

The concept that makes this statement unique among the other *omer* statements is "context." The disciples needed to understand what they had witnessed and the task Jesus was assigning them within the bigger picture of God's purposes in history. Jesus provided that picture, that context, through the Hebrew Scriptures, specifically, the Law of Moses, the Prophets, and the Psalms.

In so doing, Jesus showed His disciples that the missionary enterprise of the church is not some isolated idea, tenuously balanced on a few texts in the New Testament. No, the missionary enterprise of God's people is at the very foundation of what God cares about and has revealed from Genesis to Revelation.

We do not know all the passages Jesus pointed to in this private Bible study. We do know that God revealed His heart for the nations over and over throughout the Scriptures. Jesus may well have taken the disciples to Genesis 12 to show how God intended for all the families of the earth to be blessed through Abraham's descendants. He might have pointed out that God's purpose in giving the Torah, according to Deuteronomy 4:8, was so that all the nations might see and say, "What a great God is this, that has given this nation such statutes and righteous judgments." Perhaps He took them to Psalm 96:1–3: "Sing to the LORD a new song; sing to the LORD, all the earth. Sing to the LORD, praise his name; proclaim his salvation day after day. Declare his glory among the nations, his marvelous deeds among all peoples." And He surely must have pointed out prophetic texts that were literally fulfilled in Him. How else can we understand verse 46 of Luke 24 (NKJV), "Thus it is written, and thus it was necessary for the Christ to suffer and to rise from the dead the third day"?

Many Christians today lack the confidence to say and to show where the New Testament Scriptures claim that Jesus literally fulfilled specific Old Testament Messianic prophecies.

We must never be afraid to point to Old Testament prophecy and its fulfillment in Jesus, especially when it is so identified in the New Testament.[1] Jesus declared that the Scriptures say it was necessary for Messiah to suffer and to rise from the dead on the third day. That is the historical reality that undergirds the Great Commission.

Likewise we should speak boldly—and lovingly—of issues that many wish to avoid when it comes to witnessing. Verse 47 (NKJV) says, "Repentance and remission of sins should be preached in His name to all nations, beginning at Jerusalem."

As we proclaim the gospel, do we talk about sin and the need for people to repent? We cannot be His witnesses if we do not report faithfully the least popular part of the message, namely, the need for repentance and forgiveness of sin.

Many avoid preaching the gospel because they are afraid people will respond with anger when we say they face God's judgment if they do not receive His forgiveness for sin. But judgment is a reality and God calls us to risk people's anger so that some may be saved.

If we can catch a glimpse of the bigger picture, if we can only see how what we do and how we labor fits into the great sweep of sacred history, it will give us hope and faith and the confidence we need to press on despite discouragements and difficulties.

Y'shua wanted His disciples to see God's purposes and understand the Great Commission within the greater context of His plan for the ages. We are part of that big picture! All who hear His call—whether we are full-time missionaries or lay witnesses in our homes, schools, or workplaces—have a personal responsibility as part of that bigger picture. We are witnesses of these things.

## CONTINUITY BETWEEN
## MESSIAH'S MISSION AND OURS

The second *omer* statement Jesus made was likely during the same upper room event as the first from Luke's gospel. In this statement Y'shua said, "As the Father has sent me, I am sending you" (John 20:21).

If Luke's account looks back to the scriptural context of the Great Commission throughout the sweep of redemptive history, John looks forward, showing the continuity between our mission and that of our Messiah. John's focus is on Jesus as our model for how we are to carry out the Commission.

In what ways does Jesus sending us compare with how the Father sent His Son? We cannot mirror Jesus in all the Father sent Him to accomplish in His mission—we are not saviors. Yet we *are* to be crucified with Christ. We are not the Suffering Servant who bears the sin of the world, but we *are* sent to serve. We must identify with others as Jesus identified with us and become vulnerable as He became vulnerable. It may be easier to proclaim the gospel to people from a distance than to involve ourselves in their lives, but genuine, effective proclamation leads to personal encounters and opportunities to build relationships with unbelievers.

Some Christians have boasted, "I am really blessed. All of my friends and neighbors are Christians." Is that the kind of blessing we should seek in this life? Certainly we need to be part of the community of believers. But how can Christians fulfill our greatest responsibility if we engage only with those who know Him? In heaven, all our friends and neighbors will know the Lord. Meanwhile, our relationships ought to include those who need to hear about the Savior. Jesus prayed in John 17, "As you sent me into the world, I have sent them into the world" (John 17:18). He stated this deliberately and precisely, making His mission the model for ours.

Jesus then told His disciples to tarry in Jerusalem. He breathed on them, saying, "Receive the Holy Spirit." This foreshadowed the fuller experience of Pentecost. Along with each Great Commission statement, Jesus mentioned the power and authority of the Spirit for carrying out the work. The Great Commission formed the foundation of missionary outreach, but it was Pentecost that provided the necessary resources to fulfill it. This is in perfect keeping with Jesus' own ministry. We know from Matthew 3:16; Mark 1:10; Luke 3:22; and John 1:32 that the Spirit of God was seen descending on Jesus. With the exception of John, each gospel writer tells of the heavenly voice, indicating that the Spirit had descended because of Jesus' relationship to the Father. And John wrote concerning this, "I have seen and I testify that this [Jesus] is the Son of God" (1:34).

Just as Jesus spoke of His dependence on the Father (He only does what the Father tells Him to do, only says what the Father tells Him to say, and so on), we must realize and regularly confess our radical dependence on the Father and on the Holy Spirit whom He sent to guide and empower us. That is the only way to go forward in the manner Jesus commanded.

The gospel of John also refers to the importance of forgiveness of sin and includes an unusual statement: "If you forgive anyone his sins, they are forgiven; if you do not forgive them, they are not forgiven" (20:23). This does not mean that God either forgives or withholds forgiveness of people's sins based on our whims. Rather, as we fulfill God's Commission, we can affirm God's forgiveness for those who want to receive it on the basis of Calvary. We do not dispense His forgiveness; we announce it. We have authority to declare that sins have been forgiven when people repent and receive the message of Messiah. We also have the authority —and responsibility—to declare that there is forgiveness in no other name but Jesus. In this we maintain continuity with Jesus' words, "I am the way and the truth and the life. No one comes to the Father except through me" (John 14:6).

Too many in the church are uncomfortable with this authority. They feel it is presumption when it is actually continuity with Jesus' own message. What would be truly presumptuous is pretending we have the authority to say for- giveness may be found outside of faith in Christ. When Christ is rejected, God's forgiveness is likewise rejected. To declare this requires both the love of Messiah and also His courage. It certainly took courage for Him to say, "If you do not believe that I am the one I claim to be, you will indeed die in your sins" (John 8:24). But it is the loving thing to warn people of their future outside of Christ.

Many of us have found comfort either in saying or hear- ing it said something like, "God is the one who judges and we need to leave it in His hands. We never know what hap- pens in someone's heart." Without contradicting the truth of those two statements—because I do believe they are true— I would like to add this: We ought not to minimize the con- sequence of unbelief by pointing out how much we do not know as opposed to pointing out what we do know from the Scriptures. We need to be careful not to risk an inadvertent offer of false hope regarding those in unbelief who stand on the precipice of a Christless eternity.

As the Father sent Jesus into the world to speak His words, to do His works, and to lay down His own life for our salvation, so Jesus expects His disciples to go into the world to deliver His message. If we are faithful, we will be both loved and hated, even as Paul declared in 2 Corinthians

2:15–16, "For we are to God the aroma of Christ among those who are being saved and those who are perishing. To the one we are the smell of death leading to death; to the other, the fragrance of life. And who is equal to such a task?" Who indeed?

## CONFIDENCE THAT WE CAN DO AS HE SAID

Jesus gave His first two *omer* statements in the upper room at Jerusalem, but His third was given in Galilee as recorded in Matthew 28:16–20. In verses 16 and 17 we see how the disciples responded to the risen Lord:

> Then the eleven disciples went to Galilee, to the mountain where Jesus had told them to go. When they saw him, they worshiped him; but some doubted.

Every disciple struggles and fluctuates between worship and doubt. Do not be surprised if your belief is a continual conquest of unbelief. Our Savior commends us in our worship and commands us despite our doubt. We need confidence to worship Him and confidence to overcome doubt—confidence that Y'shua is Lord of all and that He is with us at all times. He gives us that confidence in this, perhaps the most famous of His *omer* statements:

> Then Jesus came to them and said, "All authority in heaven and on earth has been given to me. Therefore go and make disciples of all nations, baptizing them in the name of the Father and of the Son and of the Holy Spirit, and teaching them to obey everything I have commanded you. And surely I am with you always, to the very end of the age." (Matthew 28:18–20)

Do not miss the main emphasis of this command: to make disciples. A disciple is one who hears, understands, and obeys the master's teaching. A disciple of Jesus is not just a believer in Him but also a follower.

Obviously, we cannot guarantee that those who profess faith in Christ as Savior will follow on in obedience. It has been this way since New Testament times, when many professed belief and later fell away.

It is easier to focus more on helping people to the initial point of trusting in Jesus for their salvation than in helping them to follow Him as disciples. Proclaiming the gospel results in repentance and faith when the seed falls on good ground. But then, the New Testament indicates that disciples are to be baptized and instructed (see Acts 2:38, 42).

These are not divinely inspired suggestions. They are supreme challenges, and more than that, they are supreme commands uttered by the most supreme authority ever revealed to human beings by the hand of God.

So where does the confidence come in? As challenging as Y'shua's commands may be, what could possibly inspire more confidence than this promise: "Surely I am with you always, to the very end of the age" (Matthew 28:20)? This promise was a confidence booster and a great comfort for the first disciples on that mountain in Galilee so long ago. It remains so for us as we look to the promise of His return.

## CHANGE

The fourth and final *omer* statement Jesus made was just before His ascension:

Therefore, when they had come together, they asked Him, saying, "Lord, will You at this time restore the kingdom to Israel?" And He said to them, "It is not for you to know times or seasons which the Father has put in His own authority. But you shall receive power when the Holy Spirit has come upon you; and you shall be witnesses to Me in Jerusalem, and in all Judea and Samaria, and to the end of the earth." Now when He had spoken these things, while they watched, He was taken up, and a cloud received Him out of their sight. And while they looked steadfastly toward heaven as He went up, behold, two men stood by them in white apparel, who also said, "Men of Galilee, why do you stand gazing up into heaven? This same Jesus, who was taken up from you into heaven, will so come in like manner as you saw Him go into heaven." (Acts 1:6–11 NKJV)

The disciples' responses to Jesus throughout the sefirat ha-omer, that forty days between His resurrection and ascension, showed their limited understanding. They knew that He was the Messiah. They knew He had not only died but also had risen again. They no longer doubted. But they had not grasped the "so what" of Jesus' resurrection. They could not see beyond their firmly fixed understanding of what the Messiah was to do.

Jesus' fourth and final *omer* statement provides the unique perspective that change is inevitable. In order to fulfill the Great Commission, the disciples needed—just as we need—to change. Up until then, they had seen Jesus minister in a particular way and they themselves had been sent out by Him to minister, always to return to their Master after their travels.

We can hardly blame the disciples for their readiness to continue following a model that had worked well in the past. Despite everything that Jesus had said to them, despite

His death, burial, and resurrection, they assumed that model would continue in ways they could anticipate. They were mistaken. They were about to be led down paths they never imagined, to places they had never visited, where they would live and die in ways they had never envisioned.

The disciples were once again back from Galilee, outside of Jerusalem as far as Bethany (Luke 24:50). They were probably on the back side of the Mount of Olives to receive this, the final commissioning statement before Jesus ascended to heaven. We get an interesting glimpse of their final interaction with Jesus. The disciples had to be overjoyed to be reunited with Jesus. They probably had many questions. But one was uppermost in their minds:

"Lord, will you at this time restore the kingdom to Israel?" This question flowed naturally from the disciples' understanding of Jewish eschatology and the Messianic hope. They assumed the authority He had spoken of referred to His visible, tangible reign as Messiah on the throne of David.

Jesus did not deny the basis of their question. He did not say, "How dare you consider My kingdom to be a physical and literal earthly kingdom? Don't you know that it is spiritual and nonmaterial?" No, He simply stated that the information they were hoping to hear was not available to them. That was difficult for the disciples to hear then, just as it still is difficult for the church to read today.

Jesus refused to tell the apostles the future. He gave one guarantee. "You will receive power after the Holy Spirit has come upon you." Once again, we see the importance of power in evangelism, the power that comes from the indwelling Holy Spirit.

Times change. Situations change. God's Spirit moves in new ways and we must accept that as a fact of life and ministry. Jesus told His disciples that the Holy Spirit was *with* them and would be *in* them (see John 14:17). That was a powerful change from what they had experienced when Jesus was physically with them.

Once that promised power came, the disciples could fulfill their calling. Then and only then would they be equipped to be the witnesses that Y'shua (Jesus) was commissioning them to be. Before, He had sent them out two by two throughout the towns and cities of Israel, to return to Him after a short time. Now they would be sent out to people of different languages and cultures living in cities and countries they had never dreamed of. Instead of returning to Him after a short time, they would continue on until they were joined with Him in glory.

The disciples were beginning to understand Jesus, but in case they still did not "get it," He ended His earthly ministry with the greatest sermon illustration ever. While they were watching, He was taken up and a cloud received Him out of their sight. Can you imagine the looks on their faces? Maybe they started jumping up in the air and saying, "Wait a minute, Lord! We need to ask You a few more questions!" Did they know even as He disappeared that everything would change? Or did it slowly dawn on them that Jesus had left, entrusting them with a huge responsibility?

It was daunting for the disciples to face life in light of Jesus' departure, so it was important for them to receive the assurance of the angels: "Men of Galilee, why do you stand gazing up into heaven? This same Jesus, who was taken up from you into heaven, will so come in like manner as you saw Him go into heaven" (Acts 1:11 NKJV). He is coming again! That was the disciples' blessed hope, as it is ours. Yet, had Jesus not ascended, the disciples would never have fully realized their responsibilities.

Like the disciples, we have few guarantees in life. Their idea of the Messiah was based on Scripture; yet the Scriptures were fulfilled differently than they had expected. We have an idea of how Christ's return and the end times will play out—also based on Scripture. We should not be terribly surprised if God fulfills His promises differently than we expect. But like the disciples, we too have the hope that even as Jesus one day ascended into heaven, so He will one day return.

The literal, physical, visible return of Messiah Jesus should always be close to our hearts as our blessed hope and an urgent impetus for bold proclamation and intensive disciple making. What began in Jerusalem will also end in Jerusalem, with His promised return always another day closer than it ever was before. That should encourage and strengthen us as we count down to tomorrow.

Can there be any greater task? Can there be a more worthy calling in which to invest our lives? What will you be doing when Messiah's shout is heard from the heavens? When you look to the future, what do you hope to be about when that day comes? May God make us ready to stand with fresh zeal and renewed hearts and minds empowered by the Spirit of God to fulfill this Great Commission.

# LOOKING FORWARD

The biblical feasts of Israel were designed to help God's people remember what He did in the past, that we might recognize what He is doing today and have hope in His promises for tomorrow.

The "tomorrow" for those living in Old Testament times was not only the coming days, weeks, months, and years. The hope of tomorrow was also the hope of Messiah.

The "tomorrow" for those of us who have received Jesus as Messiah and Lord is divided between our future in this world—wherein we have certain promises for daily living—and our future in the world to come.

Christ is seen so significantly in the Feast of Pentecost that through Him, this holiday speaks of our past redemption as Christians, as well as to all of our tomorrows.

The original and central aspect of Pentecost is that of a firstfruits festival, with all its attendant offerings. We have seen that Paul used "first-fruits" to refer to the resurrection of Jesus. That central event pronounced the guarantee of our future resurrection as "the rest" of the harvest. Thus Pentecost helps us look back to Jesus' resurrection and forward to the day when we shall be changed and receive all the promises that God has prepared for us.

The Holy Spirit was sent, by the Father, in Christ's name on the Day of Pentecost—bringing His followers new purpose and power. We look back on that historic event, and forward to a Spirit-empowered life for our present and future on this earth as we know it. The purpose of that empowering is that we should serve God as we anticipate Christ's return. The Lord gave us a variety of guidelines on how to invest our lives until He returns—and one of the most prominent is to proclaim His gospel to others. We also know that the indwelling of the Holy Spirit is but the firstfruits of an even more intimate relationship we will one day share with Jesus when we see Him face-to-face.

We also saw how Jewish tradition transformed Pentecost into a holiday of God's Word—and how in Acts 2, the apostles' proclamation of God's Word was a dramatic demonstration that the curse at Babel had been reversed. Not only that, but the New Covenant had come into effect as people received Jesus, the living Word, into their hearts. We look back on this miraculous event and it gives us hope to look forward to an even greater day promised in Revelation 7:9: "After this I looked and there before me was a great multitude that no one could count, from every nation, tribe, people and language, standing before the throne and in front of the Lamb."

Our identities involve our past, our present, and our future, that familiar trio we have met throughout this book. At some point in the past, we were born into the world; we then had a journey of one kind or another until God met us with the gift of redemption. That is our past. Now, in a redeemed relationship with God, we are meant to live as His redeemed people, here in the present, with all the worship and service, hardships and joys that it entails. We look forward in hope to a future of resurrection, God's presence, and forever fellowship with Him and all the saints in the community of God. We don't know how the details of His promises will unfold, but we do know that our future with God is beyond anything we can comprehend.

Someday all those aspects of our lives—our identities—will come together. Our past, present, and future will converge in an integrated, healthy way. Firstfruits and Pentecost help us begin to achieve that integration now. We know from where we came—"My father was a wandering Aramean," in the words of the Pentecost liturgy in Deuteronomy 26: "He brought us to this place and gave us this land, a land flowing with milk and honey"—therefore "now I bring the firstfruits of the soil that you, O Lord, have given me." And they are just that, firstfruits, harbingers of what is yet to come.

As John says, "Dear friends, now we are children of God, and what we will be has not yet been made known. But we know that when he appears, we shall be like him, for we shall see him as he is" (1 John 3:2).

Can there be any better hope? And who would have thought that a few sheaves of wheat would have so much to teach us?

# DAILY READINGS

## DAILY OMER READINGS:
### A 49-DAY SCRIPTURE SCHEDULE
### FOR PERSONAL PENTECOST PREPARATION

**WEEK ONE**

**Theme: "Once We Were Slaves, But Now . . . "—Remembering our past so that we can serve God thankfully in the present**

**DAY 1**

As you read these two classic Old Testament passages about Pentecost, note the emphasis on the past in the Deut. passage; compare with Lev. 23:22.

Lev. 23:15–22
Deut. 16:9–12

**DAY 2**

As Paul begins his testimony in Acts 22, why does he introduce us to his past life?

Acts 22:1–10

**DAY 3**

How does the worshiper relate his previous life to his present one?

Deut. 26:1–15

**DAY 4**

How do Paul and Peter contrast the previous lives of these Christians with their present ones?

1 Cor. 6:9–11
1 Tim. 1:15–16
1 Peter 1:14–19

### DAY 5

Why do you think a sin offering is required when firstfruits are brought (v. 30)?

Num. 28:26–31

### DAY 6

How does this firstfruits occasion relate to the renewal of spiritual life in Judah?

2 Chron. 31:1–7

### DAY 7

What does God promise when we give to Him? How is this different from the "prosperity gospel"?

Prov. 3:9–10
Luke 6:38
Mark 10:28–31

## WEEK 2

**Theme: "God Has Spoken"—The place of God's Word in our lives**

### DAY 1

This is the classic OT chapter on the giving of the Law; how is God's holiness emphasized here?

Ex. 19:1–25

### DAY 2

What principles do we gather from these passages about the place of God's Word in our lives?

Luke 11:27–28
1 Peter 1:23
2 Tim. 3:16–17
Eph. 6:17
Heb. 4:12
Rev. 19:11–16

### DAY 3

What do these verses tell us about the need to teach future generations the Word of God?

Deut. 6:6
Ex. 12:26–27
Deut. 4:9
Deut. 11:19
2 Tim. 1:5
2 Tim. 3:14–15

### DAY 4

What do vv. 22–24, 39 say about Joseph and Mary's attitude toward God's Word? Compare vv. 34–35 with Heb. 4:12. Do you think

Luke 2:21–40

Jesus' growing in wisdom
has anything to do with the
Word of God? (Compare
Luke 2:41–42)

## DAY 5

| | |
|---|---|
| *Yom ha-Shoah* | Mourner's |
| On this day we break from | Kaddish |
| Pentecost readings to mourn | Ps. 102:1–28 |
| the murder of six million | Rom. 12:15 |
| Jews during the Holocaust. | Rev. 21:4 |

## DAY 6

| | |
|---|---|
| What blessings come to | Ps. 1:1–6 |
| those who follow God's | Prov. 3:13–18 |
| Word? How does our | 2 Cor. 2:14–17 |
| obedience to the Word | |
| affect others? | |

## DAY 7

| | |
|---|---|
| What are some of the ways | Ps. 119:97–112 |
| the psalmist describes the | |
| value of God's Word? | |

**WEEK 3**

**Theme: Commitment to God**

## DAY 1

| | |
|---|---|
| Ruth is traditionally read on | Book of Ruth 1 |
| Pentecost. What does this | |
| book teach about commit- | |
| ment to God and to His | |
| people? In what ways does | |
| your relationship with God | |
| reflect Ruth's? | |

**Day 2** — Book of Ruth 2

**Day 3** — Book of Ruth 3

**Day 4** — Book of Ruth 4

## DAY 5

| | |
|---|---|
| Hosea and Revelation use | Hos. 2:19–20 |
| one image for our relationship | Rev. 19:7 |
| of commitment to God; | Rev. 21:2 |
| James uses another. How does | Rev. 21:9 |
| each help you understand the | James 1:21–25 |
| nature of this commitment? | |

## DAY 6

*Yom ha-Atzma'ut*
Today is Israel Independence Day. These passages emphasize God's preservation and ultimate salvation of the Jewish people. Some Israeli congregations recite the Hallel psalms (113–18) on this day, and one such psalm is included.

Jer. 31:31–37
Rom. 11:25–27
Ps. 113:1–9

## DAY 7

This selection of verses emphasizes commitment and service to God and to one another. What principles can you glean from these verses?

Mt. 4:10
Mt. 6:24
Mark. 10:45
1 Cor. 6:19–20
Gal. 5:13
Heb. 9:14
1 Peter 4:10

## WEEK 4

**Theme: Our Life in Christ, Part I— Resurrection***

## DAY 1

Why is the resurrection so central to our Christian faith? Why is Christ's resurrection called "firstfruits"?

1 Cor. 15:12–28

## DAY 2

What is our resurrection going to be like, according to this passage? What metaphors does Paul use to explain this?

1 Cor. 15:35–57

## DAY 3

What assurances and commands did Jesus issue following His resurrection? How can you apply these to your life?

Mt. 28:1–20

## DAY 4

How does Jesus demonstrate that He is the "resurrection" in this passage?

John 11:11–45

## Day 5

How does Peter use the fact
of the resurrection to
proclaim the gospel to
his fellow Jews?

Acts 2:22–39

## Day 6

How does Paul use the
resurrection to proclaim
the gospel?

Acts 13:26–41

## Day 7

How should Jesus'
resurrection impact our
lives as Christians now?

Rom. 6:1–13

## Week 5

Theme: Our Life in
Christ, Part II—The
Holy Spirit and More

## Day 1

How does the coming of the
Holy Spirit in this chapter
relate to evangelism?
To the Old Testament?

Acts 2:1–21

## Day 2

Why does Paul say that
Christians have the "firstfruits"
of the Holy Spirit?
Why is the Holy Spirit here
called a "seal" and a "deposit"
(="down payment")?

Rom. 8:17–23
Eph. 1:3–14

## Day 3

What are some of the aspects
of our Christian hope?

Rom. 8:24–37

## Day 4

Why does Paul refer to the
first Christian converts in
these places as "firstfruits"
(literally, and in the King
James Version)? How does
that relate to the verses
regarding the harvest?

Rom. 16:5
1 Cor. 16:15–16
John 4:34–38
Mt. 9:35–38

## DAY 5

*Lag Ba'Omer*
According to tradition, a
plague against 2nd c. Rabbi
Akiva's students stopped on
this very day. The following
readings speak of another,
biblical plague. How did God
remove the plague in the OT?
What is the corresponding
"plague" in the NT and how
is it removed?

Num. 21:4–9
John 3:10–18

## DAY 6

What is the "firstfruits" here?
(See chapter 7.) What does
this say about the relationship
of Jews and Gentiles in the
church?

Rom. 11:11–33

## DAY 7

In what ways is the term
"firstfruits" used in James
and Revelation?
How did the Pentecost
holiday influence Paul's
decisions and why?
(See chapter 7.)

James 1:16–18
Rev. 14:1–5
Acts 20:16
1 Cor. 16:8–9

## WEEK 6

Theme: Anticipation
and Waiting

## DAY 1

How does this forty-day
period remind you of the
*omer* period? What was to
conclude this period of
waiting?

Acts 1:1–14

## DAY 2

What does this parable say
about readiness, anticipation,
and waiting?

Luke 12:35–48

## DAY 3

What does this passage say
about readiness and waiting
as compared to Day 2?

Mt. 24:37–51

### DAY 4

What does this passage
confirm or add to Days 2
and 3 regarding readiness
and waiting?

Mt. 25:1–13

### DAY 5

How does the Christian hope
for which we wait relate to
the OT saints mentioned here?

Heb. 11:8–16
Heb. 11:23–26
Heb. 13:13–14

### DAY 6

How should our anticipation
of Christ's return affect the
way we live now?

2 Peter 3:9–15

### DAY 7

What do these verses say
about the nature of what we
are waiting for? About our
own lives, as we wait with
anticipation?

Rom. 8:23–25
1 Cor. 1:7–9
1 Cor. 4:5
1 Thess. 1:8–10
Titus 2:11–14
James 5:7–8
Jude 21

### WEEK 7

**Theme: Our Future Life**

### DAY 1

*Yom Yerushalayim*
(Jerusalem Day)
We break from the
Pentecost readings to
commemorate the unification
of Jerusalem. What does this
psalm say about praying for
Jerusalem and for peace? What
can you pray for Jerusalem?

Ps. 122:1–9

### DAY 2

What does Isaiah say about
the future, and how does that
relate to the Spirit of God?

Isa. 11:1–10

### DAY 3

These two passages are nearly
identical. What does Micah
add? What will characterize
this future period?

Isa. 2:2–5
Mic. 4:1–7

*Daily Readings*

### Day 4

| What do these verses say about our future life in Christ? | 1 John 3:2–3<br>John 14:1–4<br>1 Cor. 2:9–10 |

### Day 5

| How does Isaiah portray the future? Can you think of a book of the NT that says something similar? | Isa. 65:17–25 |

### Day 6

| How do these verses describe our future life as individuals, and as a community? | Rev. 7:9–12<br>Rev. 21:1–7 |

### Day 7

| The *omer* period traditionally concludes with a reading of Psalm 67. How will these verses be fulfilled, according to the other readings this week? | Psalm 67:1–7 |

*Some relegate the celebration of Jesus' resurrection to Resurrection Sunday. But we continue to experience the reality of the resurrection as central to our Christian faith. This week we focus on the "firstfruits" aspect of Christ's resurrection.

# A CHRISTIAN SHAVUOT (PENTECOST) CELEBRATION

Much of the following liturgy is drawn from the rich traditions of Jewish worship and celebration, but it also expresses our faith and joy in Jesus.

*There should be two candles in holders on a table, and matches.*
*In addition, each participant needs:*
*Two loaves of bread*
*A basket of fruit*
*Some honey with a bit of bread for dipping*

## LIGHTING THE CANDLES

*Choose a woman to light the candles and recite the following prayer (in both Hebrew and English, or only in English):*

*Baruch atah Adonai, Elohenu Melech ha-olam, asher kid'shanu b'Y'shua ha-Mashiach, Or ha-olam.*

Blessed art Thou, O Lord our God, King of the universe, who has sanctified us in Y'shua the Messiah, Light of the world.

## LEADER'S INTRODUCTION

*Leader may either give spontaneous introduction or say:*

In this service we recall the Old Testament practice of offering the first of our grain, our fruit, and the work of our hands. In this visible way, we remind ourselves that God has redeemed us and that all we have is His. Let us begin with a song that pictures for us the journey of the Israelites up to Jerusalem for the festive occasions when the firstfruits were offered.

## SUGGESTED SONG: "COME LET US GO UP"[1]

## PRESENTING THE WAVE OFFERING

**Leader:** The Scriptures instructed Israel to offer the first of their crops to the Lord seven weeks after Passover, as it is written in Leviticus 23:15–22:

**Congregation:** Count off fifty days up to the day after the seventh Sabbath, and then present an offering of new grain to the Lord.

**Leader:** From wherever you live, bring two loaves made of two-tenths of an ephah of fine flour, baked with yeast, as a wave offering of firstfruits to the Lord.

**Congregation:** Present with this bread seven male lambs, each a year old and without defect, one young bull and two rams. They will be a burnt offering to the Lord, together with their grain offerings and drink offerings—an offering made by fire, an aroma pleasing to the Lord.

**Leader:** Then sacrifice one male goat for a sin offering and two lambs, each a year old, for a fellowship offering.

**Congregation:** The priest is to wave the two lambs before the Lord as a wave offering, together with the bread of the first-fruits. They are a sacred offering to the Lord for the priest.

**Leader:** On that same day you are to proclaim a sacred assembly and do no regular work. This is to be a lasting ordinance for the generations to come, wherever you live.

**Congregation:** When you reap the harvest of your land, do not reap to the very edges of your field or gather the gleanings of your harvest. Leave them for the poor and the alien. I am the Lord your God.

**Leader:** By offering these already baked loaves, we show that the work of our hands is to be offered to God.

**Congregation:** By offering the firstfruits with a burnt and sin offering, we show that sin affects the best of what we do, and that God has provided a means of atonement for our sins.

**Leader:** By offering the firstfruits with a fellowship offering, we show that offering the fruit of our hands to God is an occasion to rejoice in fellowship with Him and with one another.

**Congregation:** By leaving the gleanings of the harvest, we show that in our worship, we should always be concerned for the poor and the less fortunate.

*The congregation now lifts their loaves and waves them to symbolize offering them to the Lord.*

## PRESENTING THE *BIKKURIM* (FIRSTFRUITS)

**Leader:** Let us now recite together the confession of Deuteronomy 26:5–10.

*Congregation and leader lift up their baskets of fruit and recite:*

**All:** My father was a wandering Aramean, and he went down into Egypt with a few people and lived there and became a great nation, powerful and numerous. But the Egyptians mistreated us and made us suffer, putting us to hard labor. Then we cried out to the Lord, the God of our fathers, and the Lord heard our voice and saw our misery, toil and oppression. So the Lord brought us out of Egypt with a mighty hand and an outstretched arm, with great terror and with miraculous signs and wonders. He brought us to this place and gave us this land, a land flowing with milk and honey; and now I bring the firstfruits of the soil that you, O Lord, have given me.

**Leader:** With this confession, we remember that once we were in slavery to sin, but God redeemed us, just as He redeemed Israel from bondage in Egypt.

**Congregation:** We are a redeemed people, and we are a grateful people. And so we give God ourselves and the fruit of our labor, because He is the One who gave us life, and all that we have is His.

*Congregation and leaders deposit their baskets on a table.*

**Leader:** The firstfruits of the land remind us not only of the cycle of crops but of spiritual life and growth. For the same God who created and sustains nature has created new life in us and sustains us, through Jesus, as we read in 1 Corinthians 15:20–26:

**Congregation:** But Christ has indeed been raised from the dead, the firstfruits of those who have fallen asleep. For since death came through a man, the resurrection of the dead comes also through a man.

**Leader:** For as in Adam all die, so in Christ all will be made alive. But each in his own turn: Christ, the firstfruits; then, when he comes, those who belong to him.

**Congregation:** Then the end will come, when he hands over the kingdom to God the Father after he has destroyed all dominion, authority and power. For he must reign until he has put all his enemies under his feet.

**All:** The last enemy to be destroyed is death.

**Leader:** And until that time, Jesus lives in us through His Spirit, as we read in Romans 8:23–25:

**Congregation:** We ourselves, who have the firstfruits of the Spirit, groan inwardly as we wait eagerly for our adoption as sons, the redemption of our bodies.

**All:** For in this hope we were saved. But hope that is seen is no hope at all. Who hopes for what he already has? But if we hope for what we do not yet have, we wait for it patiently.

*Leader introduces theme of God's Word and says:*

**Leader:** In Jewish tradition, Pentecost also commemorates the giving of God's Word, the Law, on Mount Sinai. As the Lord said to Israel in Exodus 19:4–6:

**Congregation:** You yourselves have seen what I did to Egypt, and how I carried you on eagles' wings and brought you to myself. Now if you obey me fully and keep my covenant, then out of all nations you will be my treasured possession. Although the whole earth is mine, you will be for me a kingdom of priests and a holy nation.

**Leader:** As we think of the gift of God's Word to us, let us sing "Thy Word" [or alternate] and remember that His Word, the Old and New Testament, is indeed a light to our path. Not only that but the Scriptures are themselves a kind of firstfruit of the fuller communication we will have with the Lord in heaven.

## Suggested Song: "Thy Word"[2]

**Leader:** The ordinances of the Lord are sure and altogether righteous. They are more precious than gold, than much pure gold; they are sweeter than honey, than honey from the comb. (Psalm 19:9–10)

**Congregation:** How sweet are your words to my taste, sweeter than honey to my mouth! (Psalm 119:103)

**Leader:** In Jewish tradition, children are introduced to God's Word with a little honey, so that they will always associate it with sweetness. Let's dip a piece of bread in honey together and remind ourselves of the Word of God.

*All dip bread in honey and eat.*

## PSALM 67

**Leader:** Pentecost traditionally ends with the recital of Psalm 67. In reading this psalm, we are reminded that Paul refers to the first believers in the areas he visited as "firstfruits." In faith, we know that God has a fuller "crop" to be gathered from Jews and Gentiles alike. With this in mind, let's read Psalm 67 responsively:

**Leader:** May God be gracious to us and bless us and make his face shine upon us,

**Congregation:** that your ways may be known on earth, your salvation among all nations.

**Leader:** May the peoples praise you, O God; may all the peoples praise you.

**Congregation:** May the nations be glad and sing for joy, for you rule the peoples justly and guide the nations of the earth.

**Leader:** May the peoples praise you, O God; may all the peoples praise you.
**Congregation:** Then the land will yield its harvest, and God, our God, will bless us.

**All:** God will bless us, and all the ends of the earth will fear him.

## SUGGESTED SONG: *"TREES OF THE FIELD"*[3]

**Leader:** That will be a day of great rejoicing. For us, as followers of Jesus, the rejoicing has already begun. So we end on a note of joy!

## AARONIC BENEDICTION

Leader chants the benediction in Hebrew (if able) and then in English:

*Y'varech'cha Adonai v'yishm'recha.*
*Ya'er Adonai panav elecha vi-chuneka.*
*Yisa Adonai panav elecha v'yasem l'cha shalom.*

May the Lord bless you and keep you.
May the Lord make His face to shine on you and be gracious
    to you.
May the Lord lift up His countenance on you and grant you
    peace.

*Congregation can now eat the bread and fruit, or sit down to a fellowship meal.*

# RECIPES FOR SHAVUOT

## PENTECOST (SHAVUOT) RECIPES

Y ou will not find many recipes especially earmarked for the Feast of Pentecost, but you will find that dairy products and sweets are traditional fare for this holiday. And Jewish tradition offers many delicious recipes that meet both those qualifications. Blintzes and cheesecake are two of the most popular, and here you will find variations of both. The first of these recipes is reprinted from the Jews for Jesus quarterly publication *HAVURAH*; most of the others come from the *Jews for Jesus Family Cookbook*. However, you definitely do not have to be Jewish to either prepare or eat the following delicacies!

## CELEBRATING SHAVUOT IN ISRAEL
## BY DAPHNA SADAN

In Israel, at Shavuot time the children come to school dressed in white clothes. The little ones wear crowns of flowers and leaves. We decorate baskets with flowers and leaves and put in fruit as a symbol of the firstfruits that were brought to the Temple. We also fill the baskets with dairy foods like yogurt and cheese (sometimes homemade). At home, we eat meals that include dairy. On the kibbutzim, they celebrate Shavuot as an agricultural feast; they sing and dance and bring forth firstfruits of the livestock and the harvest (from *Havurah* 5.2).

Typically, a homemade yogurt cheese such as this one is enjoyed:

**Labaneh**
4 cups plain yogurt
I cup sour cream
I tsp. salt

Stir all ingredients together in large bowl. Put several layers of cheesecloth in a large colander or strainer. Place the cheese mixture on the cheesecloth and put the strainer over a larger bowl, so that it rests over it. Refrigerate overnight.

The next day, remove yogurt cheese and place it in a clean bowl. You may stir in chopped olives, green onions, chopped dried tomatoes, a little olive oil—or you may leave the cheese as is. Serve spread on crackers or bread or as a dip with fresh vegetables or fruit.

## Challah

Challah, a braided egg bread, is perhaps one of the most traditional of all Jewish foods. It accompanies the Friday night dinner that ushers in the Jewish Sabbath. Families chant a special prayer to thank God for giving us bread from the earth.

Challah is not for Sabbath only—it adds to the festivity of any meal and would be a great addition to a Pentecost celebration.

1 cup milk
6 T butter or margarine
$\frac{1}{4}$–$\frac{1}{3}$ cup sugar (use the lesser amount if you don't like your bread sweet)
1 package active dry yeast
3 eggs
1 tsp. salt
4–5 cups unbleached, all-purpose flour
1 T cold water

Bring milk, 4 tablespoons butter, and the sugar just to boil in a saucepan. Immediately remove from heat; pour into large mixing bowl and let cool to lukewarm.

Stir yeast into cooled milk mixture. Let stand for 10 minutes. It will get foamy. Beat 2 of the eggs in another small bowl. Add salt to beaten eggs; stir into milk and yeast mixture.

Stir 3 to 4 cups of flour into egg/milk mixture. Add flour 1 cup at a time, until you have a sticky dough. Sprinkle flour on a work surface and turn dough onto it. Smear the 2 tablespoons of reserved butter or margarine around the inside of a large bowl and set aside.

Sprinkle additional flour over the dough and begin kneading, adding flour as necessary. Knead until you have a smooth, nonsticky, elastic dough.

## Challah (continued)

Place dough in the greased bowl, turning dough to coat with butter. Cover top of bowl with towel and place somewhere out of a draft where the dough can rise undisturbed for 1½ hours. The dough should triple in bulk. You can test the dough by poking 2 fingers lightly in the center. If the finger holes stay depressed, and it looks like a bowling ball, it's ready.

Punch down the dough and turn it onto a floured surface. To make two loaves, cut dough into two equal parts (work with one half at a time). Cut each half into thirds. Roll out into "snakes" about 18" long. Braid snakes together; pinch ends together and tuck them under. Transfer each loaf onto a lightly greased baking sheet. Cover with a clean dish towel and let rise about 1 hour.

Preheat oven to 350°. Separate the yolk from the white of the third egg; discard or save white. Beat egg yolk with one tablespoon cold water. Lightly brush the egg and wash evenly over the loaves of bread. Set baking sheet on middle rack of oven. Bake 30 minutes (or less) until golden brown. Lightly tap with knife across top of loaf to test for doneness. It will sound hollow when done. Cool completely before eating. Makes 2 loaves.

CHRIST *in the Feast of Pentecost*

The following dressings, spreads, dips, and salads are a tasty way to begin a meal.

## Chart House Bleu Cheese Dressing

$\frac{3}{4}$ cup sour cream
$\frac{1}{2}$ tsp. dry mustard
$\frac{1}{3}$ tsp. pepper
$\frac{1}{4}$ tsp. salt
$\frac{1}{3}$ tsp. garlic powder
1 tsp. Worcestershire sauce
1 $\frac{1}{3}$ cup mayonnaise
4 oz. imported Danish bleu cheese, crumbled

In a mixing bowl combine the first 6 ingredients and blend 2 minutes with an electric mixer at low speed. Add mayonnaise and blend 30 seconds at low speed. Increase speed to medium and blend 2 minutes more. Slowly add bleu cheese and blend for 3 minutes more. Refrigerate for 24 hours before serving. Makes about 2 cups. Pour over fresh greens just prior to serving, or mix with chopped apples and nuts.

## Garlic Cheese Spread

1 stick margarine ($\frac{1}{2}$ cup)
8 oz. cream cheese, softened
2 cloves garlic, finely minced
1 tsp. dried parsley
1 tsp. Italian seasoning
Cream all ingredients together well with a wooden spoon. Store in an earthenware crock or covered bowl.
Serve with crackers. Makes about 1 $\frac{1}{2}$ cups.

## Cheese Ball

4 cups cheddar cheese, shredded

6 oz. cream cheese

$\frac{1}{3}$ cup mayonnaise

1 tsp. Worcestershire sauce

$\frac{1}{8}$ tsp. each: onion salt, garlic salt, celery salt

2 tsp. cooking sherry

Blend all together well.

Add: $\frac{1}{2}$ cup chopped, ripe olives

Chill until firm. Shape into 1 large ball or several small ones. When firm, roll in: $\frac{1}{3}$ cup fresh parsley, minced.

Wrap and chill until serving time. These cheese balls make lovely gifts.

## Garden Patch Dip

12 oz. cream-style cottage cheese

2 T each: green pepper, green onion, radishes, and carrots, chopped

$\frac{1}{2}$ tsp. salt

$\frac{1}{8}$ tsp. celery salt

$\frac{1}{8}$ tsp. dried dill weed

Combine all ingredients together well and refrigerate until serving time. Makes 2 cups. Good served with fresh, raw vegetables.

## Warm Cabbage Salad with Goat Cheese

In this recipe, the goat cheese melts into the warm salad and counters the vinegar by giving the salad a unique blend of pungent flavors.

2 oz. walnut oil

2 oz. olive oil

1 clove garlic, chopped

1 T fresh ginger, chopped

1 small head red cabbage, shredded

4 oz. balsamic vinegar

4 oz. walnuts, toasted and chopped

4 oz. goat cheese, cut into small pieces

Heat the oil in a large pot. Add the garlic and ginger and saute for 15 seconds. Add the cabbage and balsamic vinegar, and cook until the cabbage is soft but still a bit firm (about 10 minutes). Divide the cabbage onto four plates. Sprinkle the walnuts and goat cheese over the top. Makes 4 servings.

Whereas Pentecost falls just before summer, in some parts of the world it will still be chilly enough to enjoy a nice bowl of hot soup.

### Cheese and Corn Chowder

$\frac{1}{2}$ cup water

2 cups creamed corn

2 cups diced raw potatoes

$1\frac{1}{2}$ cups milk

1 cup sliced carrots

$\frac{2}{3}$ cup cheddar cheese, grated

1 cup chopped celery

1 tsp. salt

$\frac{1}{4}$ tsp. pepper

Combine first 6 ingredients in a saucepan; cover and bring to a boil. Simmer over low heat for 10 minutes. Add creamed corn and simmer 5 minutes more. Add milk and grated cheese; stir until cheese melts and chowder is heated through. Do not boil.

Makes 4–6 servings.

## Mushroom Barley Soup

3–4 pounds beef; flanken or short ribs

14 cups water

1 large onion, peeled

1 stalk celery

1 T salt

1 oz. dried mushrooms, rinsed, drained, and cut in small pieces

1½ cups onion, diced

½ cup medium pearl barley

½ cup fresh parsley, chopped

2 tsp. dried dill weed

1 cup milk

¼ cup flour

3 carrots, sliced ¼" thick

Rinse meat and put in a large pot. Add water and bring to a boil over high heat. Skim off foam and add onion, celery, and salt. Return to a boil. Lower heat; simmer, covered for 1 hour. Add dried mushrooms and simmer 30 minutes. Remove and discard onion and celery.

Add diced onion, carrots, barley, parsley, and dill weed. Simmer for 30 minutes. Remove meat to a plate. Mix milk with flour and stir into soup. Bring to a boil, reduce heat to moderately low, and simmer 10 minutes, stirring occasionally. Remove meat from bones and cut into bite-sized pieces; discard fat and bones. Return meat to soup and cook 5 minutes more. Add salt and pepper to taste.

Makes 8 servings.

## Mother-in-Law's Vegetable Barley Soup

3 qts. water

1 $\frac{1}{2}$ tsp. salt

2 chicken legs

2 chicken thighs

$\frac{1}{2}$–$\frac{3}{4}$ pound fresh string beans, cut in 1 $\frac{1}{2}$" pieces

4 small zucchini, peeled and cubed

$\frac{1}{2}$ of a small kohlrabi, peeled and cubed

2 parsnips, peeled and cubed

3 carrots, peeled and cubed

2 stalks celery, sliced thin

$\frac{2}{3}$ cup pearl barley, washed

1 onion, cut in quarters

1 cup parsley, finely chopped

1 cup parsnips tops, finely chopped

Bring water and salt to a boil in a 5-quart pot. Add remaining ingredients and bring to a boil again; lower heat, loosely cover pot, and simmer over low flame for 2 hours. Remove chicken; let cool and remove from bones; return meat to soup. Makes at least 16 cups soup.

*Note: This tastes better the second day.*

# SIDE DISHES

If you eat enough side dishes, and you want to save room for dessert, you will not need a main course—which is good because we have not offered any! With the theme of Shavuot (Pentecost) cuisine being dairy and/or sweets, we've yet to come across a special main course for this holiday. Most people we know would be quite happy to eat plenty of blintzes for their main course.

## Blintzes, of Course

This cookbook would not be complete if we didn't offer a recipe for
blintzes. These are the Jewish egg roll plus. Blintzes are to Jewish
homes what tacos are to Mexicans, a staple of life. This recipe for
blintzes comes from Ellen Zaretsky's mother. Blintzes can be fattening,
but Ellen's skinny husband, Tuvya, and their three beautiful children
don't seem to mind.

### Blintze Wrappers:

4 eggs, beaten
1 cup milk
1 cup flour
1 tsp. salt

Combine beaten eggs with milk and salt. Gradually add this mixture to
flour. Beat until smooth. Heat a heavy 6" skillet and grease lightly with
butter or margarine. Pour in only enough batter to make a very thin
pancake, tilting pan from side to side to cover bottom. Fry on 1 side
only, until blintze blisters. Turn out onto floured waxed paper, fried side
up. Repeat until all batter is used.

### Cheese Filling:

1 lb. dry-curd cottage cheese
2 T flour
2 T sugar
1 tsp. ground cinnamon

Mix together cheese, flour, sugar, and cinnamon. Place a well-rounded
tablespoon of mixture in center of blintze wrapper. Fold over both
sides toward center and roll into envelope shape. Blintzes may be
frozen at this point and browned in 350° oven when ready to serve.
Fry blintzes in butter or margarine on both sides until brown. Handle
gently. Serve with sour cream or jelly. Makes 6 servings.

## Blintze Casserole

This recipe for blintze casserole is one of our favorites, as it bypasses the process of making the individual blintze wrappers called for in traditional recipes.

### Batter:

1 cup butter, melted
3 eggs
$\frac{1}{4}$ cup milk
1 tsp. vanilla
1 cup flour
$\frac{1}{2}$ cup sugar
3 tsp. baking powder
dash salt

### Filling:

2 pounds small-curd cottage cheese
3 eggs
$\frac{1}{4}$ cup sugar
juice of 1 lemon

Mix all batter ingredients together. Mix all filling ingredients together in separate bowl. To assemble casserole: Preheat oven to 300°. Grease bottom of 2-quart baking dish. Place half of batter in baking dish. Pour in all the filling. Top with remaining batter. Bake 1 $\frac{1}{2}$ hours and serve with sour cream or jelly. Makes 8 servings.

## Aunt Maxine's Pineapple Cheese Casserole

1 (20-oz.) can chunk pineapple in its own juice, well drained (reserve juice)

$\frac{1}{4}$ cup sugar

$\frac{1}{8}$ cup flour

1 cup cheddar cheese, grated

Place pineapple in shallow, greased baking dish. Mix together sugar and flour, and sprinkle over top. Gently pour in reserved pineapple juice. Sprinkle cheese over all. Bake, uncovered, 30 minutes at 350°.
Makes 4 servings.

## Forman's Formidable Buckwheat Blinis with Caviar

These are like blintzes, but fancier and fishier. If you are put off by caviar, just leave it out (but don't leave out the sour cream on top!).

$\frac{1}{2}$ oz. yeast

$\frac{1}{2}$ cup warm water

8 oz. flour

8 oz. buckwheat flour

2 egg yolks

2 egg whites

1 T heavy cream

16 oz. smoked salmon

$\frac{1}{2}$ cup sour cream

1 oz. black or red caviar

Dissolve the yeast in the warm water. Combine yeast with the next 4 ingredients. Add the whites. Let the mixture stand in the refrigerator for 1 hour. Heat a griddle to 375°; spray with vegetable shortening. Pour out 2 ounces of batter and cook like a pancake.

Cook on 1 side until golden brown (1 minute), turn over and finish cooking (2 minutes). On a dinner plate take 4 ounces of the smoked salmon and cover the bottom of the plate. Place 3 blinis in the center of the plate and top each blini with a tsp. of sour cream and a tsp. of caviar.

Makes 16 blinis to serve 4 people.

## Toasted Cheese Ravioli

1 T olive oil
1 (9-oz.) package fresh cheese ravioli, cooked, rinsed, tossed in a little oil, chilled
½ cup red onion, chopped fine
1 (14 ½-oz.) can plum tomatoes, undrained
2 T balsamic vinegar
¼ tsp. salt
⅓ cup fresh basil, chopped (or 1 T dried basil)
grated Parmesan

Heat oil in large skillet over high heat. Add ravioli, making sure to separate any that stick together. Toast on both sides until crisp-tender, about 4 minutes. Remove from pan and set aside. Add onions to pan (with a little water if necessary, to keep from sticking). Stir-fry until heated, about 2 minutes. Add tomatoes and their liquid, vinegar, and salt. Bring to a boil for about 2 minutes. Add ravioli; stir-fry 30 seconds. Add basil. Toss well and serve with grated Parmesan. Makes 4 servings.


## Cheese Latkes

This is a variation on potato latkes, a favorite Hanukkah treat.

3 eggs, well beaten
1 cup milk
½ tsp. cinnamon
1 T sugar
1 cup pot cheese or dry-curd cottage cheese
1 cup matzah meal

Combine eggs, milk, cinnamon, sugar, and cheese in a large bowl. Add matzoh meal until mixture is fairly dry. Drop by tablespoons onto a well-greased frying pan or griddle; brown on both sides. Serve with sour cream, applesauce, or jelly. Makes approximately 16 pancakes.

## Noodle Cheese Pudding

1 (16-oz.) package broad noodles
$\frac{1}{2}$ tsp. salt
3 eggs
4 T butter or margarine
1 (8-oz.) package cream cheese
$\frac{1}{2}$ cup cottage cheese

Cook noodles according to package directions; drain. Add salt and eggs to noodles in large bowl; mix well. Heat butter or margarine in large frying pan; add half of the cooked noodles; then make a layer of each of the cheeses and cover with the rest of the noodles. Let pudding cook until brown over medium heat; then turn it over (like a huge pancake) and let cook until brown on other side.
Makes 5–6 servings.

# DESSERTS

Anything that is cheesy, creamy, and/or sweet will do nicely as a dessert for a celebratory Pentecost meal. Here are a few you might like to try.

---

### Fruity Low-Fat Cheesecake

This is the first and last low-fat dessert we will mention. Feel free to make (or buy) your favorite high-fat cheesecake as well.

1 cup All-Bran cereal (reduced to crumbs in food processor or blender)

$\frac{1}{4}$ cup diet or light margarine, melted

2 (15-oz.) containers light ricotta cheese

$\frac{1}{2}$ cup liquid nondairy creamer

$\frac{1}{2}$ cup sugar

2 T flour

1 T lemon juice (fresh, if possible)

1 tsp. each grated fresh lemon and orange peel

$\frac{1}{4}$ tsp. salt

2 eggs (or 3 egg whites)

fresh fruit, sliced

Prepare crust by mixing together crushed cereal and melted margarine; press into bottom and sides of 8" or 9" spring form pan (if spring form pan is not available, use round Pyrex or Corning Ware dish). Put crust in refrigerator. In large bowl add all remaining ingredients, except eggs and fruit. Beat well with electric mixer until smooth. Add eggs (or whites), one at a time, until smooth. Pour batter over crust. Bake in preheated 350° oven for 60 minutes or until center is firm. Shut off oven. Cool in oven with door slightly ajar for 30 minutes. Chill 3 hours in refrigerator and top with fresh sliced fruit (kiwi and strawberries are nice).

Makes 10 servings.

## Last-Minute Sour Cream Pie

This recipe is one of the easiest, most successful desserts you'll ever make. If you are making the rest of your meal with the more complicated "from scratch" recipes, do yourself a favor and choose this one for the dessert!

1 8-inch graham cracker crust, store-bought
1 cup sour cream
1 cup milk
1 (3 $\frac{1}{2}$-oz.) package instant pudding*

Beat sour cream with milk until smooth. Blend in pudding mix until smooth and slightly thickened. Pour into graham cracker crust and chill 1 hour or until set. If desired, serve with whipped cream.
Makes 6 servings.

*vanilla (for the basic recipe) or butterscotch pudding
  banana pudding—add sliced bananas on top of pie
  chocolate pudding—garnish top with chocolate shavings

## Traditional Jewish Rugelach

These wonderful little rolled cookies are not quick or easy but DELI-CIOUS! Oh yes!

1 pound sweet, unsalted butter
8 oz. cream cheese (can be the low-fat variety)
3 $\frac{1}{2}$ cups flour
3 T sour cream (can also be reduced-fat)
$\frac{1}{4}$ cup sugar
pinch salt
16 oz. apricot or strawberry jam, or marmalade
$\frac{1}{2}$ cup walnuts, finely chopped

Cream together butter and cream cheese. Add flour, sour cream, sugar, and salt. Knead well to form a stiff dough. Refrigerate for several hours until firm. Roll into 9" circles, using about $\frac{1}{8}$ of the dough for each circle. Combine jam or marmalade with chopped walnuts and spread on each circle. Cut each circle into 8 wedge-shaped sections. Roll each wedge, starting from the large end and ending with the point. Curve to form a crescent, placing open end down on a buttered baking sheet. Bake at 375° for 15 minutes or until browned. Makes 4 dozen.

## Baklava (a Middle Eastern Specialty)

If you've ever eaten in a Middle Eastern restaurant, be it Greek, Persian, Israeli, or Arabic, you may have seen baklava on the dessert menu. At one time it was unthinkable for the average American to try making this delicacy, as it requires a special, extremely thin dough called phyllo. Perhaps there are still some patient cooks out there who make their own phyllo leaves. We do not happen to know anyone like this, but we do know packaged phyllo can be found in many super-markets these days.

1 pound walnuts, finely ground
$\frac{1}{2}$ cup sugar
2 tsp. cinnamon
$\frac{1}{8}$ tsp. ground cloves
$\frac{1}{4}$ cup finely ground fresh bread crumbs
1 pound phyllo leaves, defrosted according to package instructions
1 pound sweet, unsalted butter, melted (with foam skimmed off top)

## Syrup:

2 cups sugar
1 cup honey
2 cups water
1 tsp. cinnamon
2 whole cloves
1 tsp. lemon juice

In small bowl, combine walnuts, sugar, cinnamon, cloves, and bread crumbs. Brush 12"x17"x1" baking sheet with melted butter.
Place 6 phyllo leaves on bottom, brushing each one with melted but-ter as you go. Spread $\frac{1}{2}$ cup walnut mixture over these layers.
Repeat with remaining leaves and nut mixture, reserving about 6 leaves for the top. Brush top with remaining melted butter.
With a sharp, pointed knife, score the top sheets in small diamond or square shapes. Bake in 350° oven for 35–45 minutes, until golden brown but not burnt around the edges. Let cool completely.
Heat together syrup ingredients in medium saucepan until warm and

*CHRIST in the Feast of Pentecost*

## Baklava (a Middle Eastern Specialty) (continued)

well-blended. Remove the cloves and pour warm syrup evenly over top of baklava. Allow to cool for 1 day before eating.

Makes 20–25 servings, depending on how you cut the layers.

*Note: Phyllo leaves can be tricky to work with—they dry out quickly if left uncovered. After defrosting leaves, unroll on clean dish towel and cover with another clean towel. Keep leaves covered as you work, and try to work quickly.*

## Viv's Baklava Rolls

2 ½ cups sugar

2 cups water

¼ cup honey

juice of ½ orange or 1 tsp. orange extract

1 pound phyllo leaves

½ pound sweet, unsalted butter, melted

5 cups walnuts, chopped

2 ½ tsp. ground cinnamon

1 tsp. ground cloves

Boil together sugar, water, and honey until slightly thickened over medium heat; add orange juice or extract and let cool. Take 2 sheets phyllo dough and place in greased jelly roll pan or cookie sheet. Brush lightly with melted butter. Mix together chopped walnuts and spices. Spread ½ cup nut mixture at one end of dough; turn in long ends and roll gently. Place, ends down, in pan. Repeat with remaining sheets (double the sheets) until nut mixture is used up. Refrigerate, then slice diagonally into 1 ½"–2" pieces. Bake at 325° for 25 minutes. Makes 20 servings.

## Mount Sinai Cake

Jewish tradition tells us that God gave the Torah at Mount Sinai on the Day of Pentecost. This cake is a delicious reminder of that event. You can find various recipes for Mount Sinai Cake; some are very elaborate. This one is easy and fun for kids (let them help you decorate it). We found it online at: www.babaganewz.com/kidspdfs/mtSinaiCake.pdf

### You'll need:

1 box of your favorite cake mix, any flavor
1-liter oven-safe bowl, such as Pyrex
1 cup green icing (or white icing with a few drops of food coloring added)
$\frac{1}{2}$ cup assorted jelly beans
1 cup whipped cream
$\frac{1}{2}$ cup red-colored granulated sugar

### Instructions:

Prepare the cake mix according to package instructions. Place the batter in a 1-liter oven-safe bowl, such as a Pyrex bowl. (NOTE: If there is too much batter to leave room for the cake to rise in the bowl, leave out some of the batter.) Bake the cake.

Allow the cake to cool in the bowl. Once it is cool, turn it out onto a serving platter so it looks like a mountain.

Frost the cake with green icing. This represents the greenery on the mountain. "There was grass around Mount Sinai" (*Mishnah Berurah* 494:10).

Surround the base of the cake with assorted jelly beans. These represent the Jewish people.

Set 1 jelly bean on the very top of the mountain. This represents Moses who went up Mount Sinai alone.

## Mount Sinai Cake (continued)

Put a crown of whipped cream on the tip of the cake (covering the jelly bean). This represents the cloud that engulfed the mountain.

Sprinkle the red-colored sugar over the green icing. This represents the fire of God that descended onto the mountain just before God gave us the Torah.

Enjoy!

# LAW, GRACE, AND TRADITION

It is one thing to appreciate how Pentecost points to Jesus and to spiritual truths for our Christian lives. Some may feel it is quite another, however, to consider *practicing* anything that seems based in the Old Testament and/or tradition (such as the Pentecost liturgy provided in this book). Christians rightly want to be certain they are not "going back under the law."

## THE NEW COVENANT AND THE LAW OF MOSES

The authors of this book (and most evangelical Christians) recognize that we are now under the New Covenant, rather than the Mosaic Covenant (Law of Moses). This New Covenant is described in Jeremiah 31:31–34; Luke 22:20; 1 Corinthians 11:25; 2 Corinthians 3:6; Hebrews

8:8; 9:15; 12:24. With the New Covenant in effect, the Law of Moses as a "package" is not mandated for believers in Jesus, whether Jewish or Gentile. Nor is it possible, even if one desired it, to observe all of the 613 commandments of the Law of Moses. Many of these laws pertain to Temple worship or to priests, which no longer exist. Some pertain to specific aspects of life in the land of Israel and cannot be kept by those outside the land (which not only includes the vast majority of Gentiles but also still includes a majority of Jews in the world).

However, Christians throughout history have also recognized that the New Covenant by no means reflects any change in God's character. His commandments, even the ceremonial ones, expressed that character—His holiness, His goodness, His justice, and so much more. Further, the commandments expressed His desire for how we should relate to Him. God's character and standards are still His "law" for us, inasmuch as we are to measure our attitudes and behavior against His holiness, goodness, justice, and so on.

How that works out in practice sometimes differs under the New Covenant, but in some cases, it may be the same as it was in the Law of Moses. For example, Deuteronomy 24:17 says, "Do not deprive the alien or the fatherless of justice." That remains as true today as it was over three thousand years ago. However, in the same chapter, verse 20 reads, "When you beat the olives from your trees, do not go over the branches a second time. Leave what remains for the alien, the fatherless and the widow." Relatively few of us have olive trees to beat, nor do we see many aliens (resident strangers), orphans, and widows go through fields to glean the leftovers as they did in Bible times. But certainly we should adhere to the principle and translate it into modern terms.

It should be noted that the Law of Moses was never a

means of salvation. No one was or ever could be saved except by the grace of God. Rather, the Law was given following Israel's "salvation," i.e., redemption from slavery in Egypt. It underscored the fact that the Hebrew people were under a new Lord—not Pharaoh but the God of Israel. As *His* servants they were bound to carry out *His* will. Further, the Law was meant to be lived not only in obedience but also gratitude to God. The same is true under the New Covenant. Whatever obedience God requires or desires from us is not the basis for our salvation but to express our relationship to Him.

## THE VALUE OF THE LAW

Some leading figures in church history have realized that God's Law has value for Christians today. Traditionally this value has been referred to as the "three uses" of the Law, as formulated by sixteenth-century reformer John Calvin. The three uses are (1) to convict nonbelievers of their sin and lead them toward Christ; (2) to restrain wrongdoing in society at large, and so benefit the public community; and (3) the "principal use," as a guide to the Christian life.[1]

These uses were specifically applied to the "moral law," embodied largely in the Ten Commandments, but in reality even the ceremonial commandments were also "moral" because they reflected God's character and many of them demonstrated that our breach of His righteous ways could only be rectified on His terms. For example, we know the laws concerning sacrifice were fulfilled in the final atoning sacrifice of Jesus. We need not, and ought not, sacrifice animals for the forgiveness of our sins. But the principles of old —acknowledging our sin, repenting, and trusting in God's provision alone (Jesus)—remain the same.

As we have seen in this book, the commandment to bring the firstfruits of one's crops reflected on God as the One who redeemed Israel and brought them into a land of bounty; it reflected our responsibility to be grateful to God. It also showed the need to trust the God of Israel and not the gods of Canaan, even through the perils of the growing season. These matters of faith and morals are embodied in a particular ceremony that is certainly no longer binding on us, yet the ceremony points to principles that we ought to remember and apply.

Therefore while we are not bound to the Law of Moses as the *specific expression* of God's will, it has great value.

How then can a Christian avail himself or herself of the value of the Law? One way is to recognize that the Law is indeed a teacher and a guide to principles God wants us to reflect in our lives. For that reason, many churches celebrate "Christian Passover seders" to instruct people on how Jesus fulfilled Passover and to enhance their worship by remembering that He is our Passover (1 Corinthians 5:7) and the Lamb of God (John 1:29). For many Christians, such a seder also enriches Communion. It can also help Christians better understand and converse with their Jewish friends and neighbors. We offer a Pentecost worship ceremony for Christians in appendix B for similar reasons. No obligation for Christians to observe the Law of Moses should be inferred from its inclusion in this book, as it was designed to glorify Jesus and to aid in teaching and worship.

## TRADITIONS

Some have raised questions about the value of human tradition in our worship. Why should we pay attention to customs (regarding Pentecost or anything else) that did not originate in the Bible?

First of all, every culture and every church has certain traditions that are neither given in Scripture, nor contrary to Scripture. Such traditions might include a particular prayer or song before or after the offering, a particular format for celebrating Communion (passing it throughout the pews, dispensing it at the altar, etc.), a church steeple with bells, or a monthly potluck. In fact, if we were to list all the traditions of our churches, families, and communities, "I suppose that even the whole world would not have room for the books that would be written." Communities of worship can no more be tradition-free than music can be sound-less.

Not all traditions are equal: they can be helpful or harmful. Some promote godliness, others hinder it. About the latter, Jesus remarked, "You have a fine way of setting aside the commands of God in order to observe your own traditions!" (Mark 7:9). On the other hand, in Luke 4:16, "He went to Nazareth, where he had been brought up, and on the Sabbath day he went into the synagogue, as was his custom. And he stood up to read." Jesus took part in the traditional weekly reading in the synagogue though the tradition was not from the Law of Moses, for there were no synagogues then.

The "four cups" that Jewish people partake of during the Passover seder did not originate in the Old Testament. Yet by the time Jesus celebrated the festival with His disciples, the cups were part of the Passover tradition. Moreover, Jesus used that tradition to unveil something earthshaking about Himself and His mission: "In the same way, after the supper he took the cup, saying, 'This cup is the new covenant in my blood, which is poured out for you'" (Luke 22:20).

In this book, we have also seen how God used Jewish traditions concerning Pentecost in Acts 2, and how Peter did the same in his preaching, when he spoke about Jesus and the Holy Spirit.

It is interesting to note that Paul and almost all the other Jewish Christians of the first century maintained their traditions and observant service of the Law of Moses (Acts 21:20). Perhaps it took time for them to realize the implications of the fact that Jesus' death had ushered in the New Covenant. Most likely, accustomed as they were to the laws and traditions, it would have been difficult to abandon these practices —and unnecessary, as long as they did not impose them on one another. Paul's admonition regarding such things surely applies here: "Each one should be fully convinced in his own mind" (Romans 14:5).

So today, we are free to practice traditions that do not conflict with the teaching of Scripture—not to win favor with God but rather to help us learn of Him, love Him, serve Him, and worship Him.

## WHAT ABOUT GRACE?

Some use John 1:17 to show the Law is of comparatively little value now that we are in a new era: "For the law was given through Moses, but grace and truth were realized through Jesus Christ." In actuality, this verse compares Moses (who was only an agent through whom God gave the law) to Jesus (the creator, through whom grace and truth came into being).

Others speak of "law versus grace" with the idea that in Old Testament times life was burdensome because of the Law, while in New Testament times there is a freedom not found in the Old Testament. The New Testament does contrast law and grace but not quite in that way.

The New Testament argues against the misconception that we can be justified through the Law (Acts 13:38–39). Believers in Jesus are not "under law," meaning the Law of

Moses does not have authority over us. But it would be quite wrong to suggest that grace and freedom were lacking in Old Testament times, or that God's law made life heavy or burdensome. Jesus pointed out that later, man-made traditions constituted a burden to many (Matthew 23:4), but God's laws are not so. Psalm 19 tells how wonderful the Law is to the psalmist; it shows him right and wrong and how to live a meaningful life. Thus the Law gives him freedom to live as he should (see above on the third "use" of the Law).

While we may be free from the various statutes and ordinances of the Law of Moses, that freedom is to be balanced by our love for God and one another (Romans 13:8; Galatians 5:14), with the accompanying responsibilities to follow the leading of the Holy Spirit, translate our faith into day-to-day practice, and seek to obey God in all areas of our lives. In some ways this can be more challenging than it was under the Law of Moses!

## A FINAL WORD

Participating in Old Testament–based ceremonies and Jewish traditions is an option, not a requirement, for believers in Jesus, whether Jewish or non-Jewish. Jewish believers may feel more comfortable integrating some of those traditions and ceremonies into their lives, since many are familiar. Those who are not Jewish may not feel any need to incorporate them into their worship, while others might want to do so to enhance their worship. As 1 Corinthians 10:31 says, "So whether you eat or drink or whatever you do, do it all for the glory of God."

# SUGGESTED READING LIST

Goodman, Philip. *The Shavuot Anthology*. Philadelphia: Jewish Publication Society, 1992. A delightful and instructive collection containing everything someone could possibly want to know about Shavuot, from the Bible and Jewish writings to modern short stories and poems, to liturgy, humor, recipes, and music.

Isaacs, Ronald H. *Every Person's Guide to Shavuot*. Northvale, NJ: Jason Aronson, 1998.

Strassfeld, Michael. *The Jewish Holidays: A Guide and Commentary*. New York: Harper & Row, 1985. Pages 47–83 deal with the *omer* period and Shavuot from the vantage point of contemporary Judaism.

Waskow, Arthur I. *Seasons of Our Joy: A Modern Guide to the Jewish Holidays*. Boston: Beacon Press, 1990, © 1982. Pages 164–205 cover this holiday; also from the viewpoint of contemporary Judaism.

# NOTES

## Chapter 1: What's in a Name?

1. For details, see *Theological Wordbook of the Old Testament*, ed. R. Laird Harris, Gleason L. Archer, and Bruce K. Waltke (Chicago: Moody, 1980), vol. 1262.

2. *Shavuot* is plural; the singular is *shavua*. See Ibid., vol. 2, 899.

3. Ronald H. Isaacs, *Every Person's Guide to Shavuot* (Northvale, NJ: Jason Aronson, 1998), 16.

4. For more information, see *Christ in the Feast of Tabernacles*, Moody, ©2005, by David Brickner.

## Chapter 2: Pentecost in the Old Testament

1. Later, Jewish tradition linked Pentecost with the giving of the Law.

2. Later on, Purim is also linked to history in the book of Esther. Between the testaments, Hanukkah recalls the victory of the Maccabees in 165 B.C.

3. See *Theological Wordbook of the Old Testament*, ed. R. Laird Harris, Gleason L. Archer, and Bruce K. Waltke (Chicago: Moody, 1980), vol. 1, 109 and vol. 2, 826.

4. Nogah Hareuveni, "The Seven Species of the Land of Israel," *Jewish Heritage Online Magazine*, http://www.jhom.com/topics/seven/species.html.

5. Joseph Gutmann, "Haggadah Art," 139, in *Passover and Easter: The Symbolic Structuring of Sacred Seasons* (*Two Liturgical Traditions*, vol. 6), ed. Paul F. Bradshaw and Lawrence A. Hoffman (Notre Dame, IN: University of Notre Dame Press, 1999).

6. See a similar idea in Efrat Zarren-Zohar, "From Passover to Shavuot," 71–93, especially 74–75, ibid.

7. Gordon J. Wenham, *The Book of Leviticus*, New International Commentary on the Old Testament (Grand Rapids: Eerdmans, 1979), 57–63. See Leviticus 1:4 on the idea of atonement in the burnt offering.

8. Ibid., 92–93.

9. Bruce K. Waltke, *The Book of Proverbs*, New International Commentary on the Old Testament (Grand Rapids: Eerdmans, 2005), vol. 1, 107–109. The material in this section is indebted to Waltke's discussion on those pages and also on pp. 103–104.

10. That is not an argument against working to relieve poverty and persecution, however!

11. 2 Chronicles 31:5; Nehemiah 10:35; 12:44; 13:31; Proverbs 3:9; Ezekiel 44:30.

## Chapter 3: Forty–Nine Days of Purpose?

1. With the exception of the Karaites (9th c. A.D.) and the Falashas (modern times).

2. *The Book of Jubilees*, written about the 2nd c. B.C., suggests the Pentecost-Law connection may have existed then; see 1:1 and chapter 6.

3. Arthur I. Waskow, *Seasons of Our Joy: A Modern Guide to the Jewish Holidays*. (Boston: Beacon Press, 1990, © 1982), 187.

4. Ibid., 167.

5. Ibid., 168.

6. In the Talmud, see *Yevamot* 62b (this can be found in the *Soncino Talmud*, the standard English translation of the Talmud, vol. 6, 417); in the Midrash, *Genesis Rabbah* 61:3; *Ecclesiastes Rabbah* 11:6 (these can be found in the *Midrash Rabbah* published by Soncino, the standard English translation, respectively in vol. 2, 542 and vol. 8, 294–95).

7. Eliezer Segal, *Holidays, History, and Halakhah* (Northvale, NJ: Jason Aronson, 2000), 187.

8. Or beginning with Lag Ba'Omer, some suspend mourning just *on* the day, others *beginning with* the day.

9. Ronald H. Isaacs, *Every Person's Guide to Shavuot* (Northvale, NJ: Jason Aronson, 1998), 18.

10. This is not to spiritualize away the literal promises God made to Israel of

the land. It is clear, however, that the New Testament applies them to our Christian lives.

11. Michael Strassfeld, *The Jewish Holidays: A Guide and Commentary*, (New York: Harper & Row, 1985), 48.

## Chapter 4: Celebrating Pentecost: Customs and Traditions

1. For further details, see Eliezer Segal, *Holidays, History, and Halakhah* (Northvale, NJ: Jason Aronson, 2000), 212–14; Michael Strassfeld, *The Jewish Holidays: A Guide and Commentary* (New York: Harper & Row, 1985), 71–77; Ronald H. Isaacs, *Every Person's Guide to Shavuot* (Northvale, NJ: Jason Aronson, 1998), 13–39, 65–77; Philip Goodman, *The Shavuot Anthology* (Philadelphia: Jewish Publication Society, 1992), 83–101, 229–37.

2. Arthur I. Waskow, *Seasons of Our Joy: A Modern Guide to the Jewish Holidays*, (Boston: Beacon Press, 1990, © 1982), 192; Michael Strassfeld, *The Jewish Holidays: A Guide and Commentary* (New York: Harper & Row, 1985), 73.

3. Arthur Waskow translates as "Repair of the Night of Shavuot" (Waksow, *Seasons of Our Joy*, 192). For both meanings, see the two articles on "tikkun" in *The Encyclopedia of the Jewish Religion*, eds. R. J. Zwi Werblowsky and Geoffrey Wigoder (New York, Chicago, San Francisco: Holt, Rinehart and Winston, 1965), 384–85.

4. *The Zohar*, 2nd ed., vol. 5, trans. by Harry Sperling and Maurice Simon, (London; New York: Soncino Press, 1984, 123 [section *Emor*]).

5. Ronald H. Isaacs, *Every Person's Guide to Shavuot*, 70; Michael Strassfeld, *The Jewish Holidays, A Guide and Commentary*, 73.

6. Hayyim Schauss, *The Jewish Festivals: History and Observance*, trans. Samuel Jaffe (New York: Schocken Books, 1962, 1938), 95.

7. For a very good brief treatment, see Francis A. Schaeffer, *Art and the Bible* (Downers Grove, IL: InterVarsity, 1973).

8. *The Jewish Catalog*, vol. 1, ed. Richard Siegel, Michael Strassfeld, and Sharon Strassfeld (Philadelphia: Jewish Publications Society of America, 1973), 147–48.

9. Goodman, *The Shavuot Anthology*, 250.

10. Ibid., 248.

11. A tradition concerning *kreplach*: it is said that the three corners representing the three portions of the *Tanach* (Hebrew Scriptures), which are *Torah* (the Law), *Neviim* (the Prophets), and *Ketuvim* (the Writings). The three corners can also be said to represent the trifold nature of Israel: the priests, the Levites, and the people. Further, the three corners can represent Moses, who was the third born in his family (Goodman, *The Shavuot Anthology*, 250, referencing Shabbat 88a in the Babylonian

Talmud), as well as Sivan, which is the third month of the Jewish calendar in which Pentecost falls. (Shabbat 88a) Of course Christians can see an additional meaning in the number three as we reflect on the triune nature of God.

12. Goodman, *The Shavuot Anthology*, 251.

13. Exodus 3:8, 17; 13:5; 33:3; Leviticus 20:24; Numbers 13:27; 14:8; 16:13, 14; Deuteronomy 6:3; 11:9; 26:9, 15; 27:3; 31:20; Joshua 5:6; Jeremiah 11:5; 32:22; Ezekiel 20:6, 15. A twenty-first instance is different: "Your lips drop sweetness as the honeycomb, my bride; milk and honey are under your tongue" (Song of Songs 4:11).

14. Strassfeld, *The Jewish Holidays*, 73; Goodman, *The Shavuot Anthology*, 249.

15. Hayyim Schauss, *The Jewish Festivals*, 94.

16. Goodman, *The Shavuot Anthology*, 246.

17. Goodman, *The Shavuot Anthology*, 87; Strassfeld, *The Jewish Holidays*, 72.

18. Goodman, *The Shavuot Anthology*, 87

19. Strassfeld, *The Jewish Holidays*, 72

20. Ibid.

21. This theme is part of other holidays too: On *Rosh Hashanah*, the Jewish New Year, apples and honey are eaten to express the wish for a sweet new year. At Passover, the apple-and-spice mixture known as *charoset* reminds us, according to some traditions, of the sweetness of redemption.

22. Other names for the papercuts are *shoshanta* (roses) or *shevusolekh* ("little Shavuot").

23. For the last two paragraphs, see Waskow, *Seasons of Our Joy*, 199–200; see also Goodman, *The Shavuot Anthology*, 157, 159.

24. Exodus 12 enjoins teaching children about the Exodus and God's redemption. Again, many of the themes of Shavuot span other holidays as well.

25. 2:21–22 in Hebrew.

26. Reform Jews call their house of worship a Temple rather than a synagogue.

27. The poem is actually in Aramaic, a close cousin to Hebrew that uses the same alphabet.

28. Translation from Avie Gold, *The Complete Artscroll Machzor: Shavuos* (Brooklyn: Mesorah Publications, 1991), 271, 273.

29. Many scholars see in the Tabernacle, in the Temple, and in the land of Israel itself pictures of the Garden of Eden, as if to say that redemption will restore what we lost in Paradise.

30. The story is recounted in many places. See for instance, Kenneth W. Osbeck, *101 Hymn Stories* (Grand Rapids: Kregel, 1982), 127–28.

31. Philip Goodman, *The Shavuot Anthology* (Philadelphia: Jewish Publication Society, 1992), 90, in the translation by Theodor H. Gaster.

## Chapter 5: Pentecost in the Gospels

1. The Mishnah (ca. A.D. 200) contains material relating both to pre-A.D. 70 life as well as life in the second century. The tractate of the Mishnah cited here, *Bikkurim*, describes the bringing of firstfruits whether at Pentecost or at other times of the year.

2. Mishnah *Bikkurim* 3:3–4, 6, 8, in the *Soncino Talmud* edition, in *Seder Zera'im*, second half, 400–401.

3. It is perhaps coincidental, but in Jewish tradition Shavuot is the time of judgment on trees: "According to the Mishnah (Rosh Hashanah 1:2), it is on Shavuot that the trees and their fruits are judged by God, who decides whether the year will be one of abundance or scarcity. This judgment will affect the quality of the firstfruits that are brought to the Temple" (Isaacs, *Guide to Shavuot*, 73). If this tradition in fact goes back to the first century, which is hard to determine, there may have been an additional factor in the timing of Jesus' act.

4. J. N. Geldenhuys, *Commentary on the Gospel of Luke: The English Text with Introduction, Exposition and Notes*, New International Commentary on the New Testament (Grand Rapids: Eerdmans, 1975, 1951), 201, accepts the phrase and relates it to the second sabbath after Nissan 15, the first Sabbath falling in Passover week itself. Similar interpretations are given in the older works by John Lightfoot (*A Commentary on the New Testament from the Talmud and Hebraica*, vol. 2, (Peabody, MA: Hendrickson, reprint 1979), 193 ff., and according to Geldenhuys, in Strack-Billerbeck (a standard German-language commentary on the New Testament from the rabbinic writings) as well. On the other hand, Walter Wessel in the *Expositor's Bible Commentary*, vol. 8 (Grand Rapids: Zondervan, 1984) allows that if the reading were original, a "second sabbath" meaning is plausible; but he inclines against accepting it (p. 888). I. Howard Marshall (*The Gospel of Luke*, New International Greek Testament Commentary [Grand Rapids: Eerdmans, 1978]) seems to reject the phrase altogether as a scribal addition (p. 230). If "the second sabbath after the first" is accepted as the original reading, some take it to mean the second major sabbath incident that Luke mentions in his gospel, the first being in 4:31. The interpretation given in this book is certainly plausible, but we cannot be certain.

## Chapter 6: The Day Pentecost Was Fulfilled

1. Fragment-Targum (from the Cairo Geniza) to Exodus 20:2, as cited in Joseph B. Fuiten, *The Revenge of Ephesus*, 124, n. 256. Available at www.Cedarpark.org/resources/books/books/Revenge_of_ephesus.pdf.

2. As cited in Fuiten, *Revenge of Ephesus*, 123–24, n. 255.

3. Fuiten, *The Revenge of Ephesus*, 123, n. 254, citing Old Kvarme, *The Acts of the Apostles* (Jerusalem: Caspari Center for Biblical and Jewish Studies, 1994), 10.

4. *Mekilta de-Rabbi Ishmail*, tr. Jacob Lauterbach, vol. 2 (Philadelphia: Jewish Publication Society, 1976, © 1933), 266.

5. Ibid., 267

6. *Exodus Rabbah*, V. 9, 87, in the *Soncino Midrash Rabbah* edition.

7. *Exodus Rabbah* v. 9 (*Midrash Rabbah: Exodus*, tr. S. M. Lehrman; (London, New York: Soncino Press, 3rd ed., 1983), 86

8. Ronald H. Isaacs, *Every Person's Guide to Shavuot* (Northvale, NJ: Jason Aronson, 1998) 70; Michael Strassfeld, *The Jewish Holidays: A Guide and Commentary* (New York: Harper & Row, 1985), 73.

## Chapter 7: More Reflections on Firstfruits from the New Testament

1. 2 Timothy 2:3–4.

2. 1 Corinthians 9:26–27.

3. 1 Corinthians 9:24; Galatians 5:7; 2 Timothy 4:7.

4. 1 Corinthians 3:7–8; Galatians 6:9.

5. Colossians 2:15.

6. 1 Corinthians 12:12–27.

7. 1 Thessalonians 2:7.

8. Pronounced *ap-ar-kay;* does not rhyme with "Apache"!

9. G. M. Burge, "Firstfruits, Down Payment," in *Dictionary of Paul and His Letters*, ed. Gerald F. Hawthorne and Ralph P. Martin (Downers Grove, IL: InterVarsity, 1993), 300.

10. N. T. Wright, *The Resurrection of the Son of God*, (Christian Origins and the Question of God, vol. 3 (Minneapolis: Fortress Press, 2003), 337–38.

11. Burge, 301.

12. Though it is possible to "grieve" the Holy Spirit through sin, says Paul (Ephesians 4:30). But God does not speak of "removing" His Spirit from us, as we sometimes read in regard to Old Testament personages.

13. Romans 9:4–5.

14. Throughout Romans 9–11.

15. Romans 11:1–5.

16. "By 'their rejection' must be meant their temporary casting away by God, which is here, it seems, thought of as identical with, rather than as consequential on, their refusal of the Messiah"—C. E. B. Cranfield, *Romans: A Shorter Commentary* (Grand Rapids: Eerdmans, 1985), 276.

17. See Douglas J. Moo, *The Epistle to the Romans*, New International Commentary on the New Testament (Grand Rapids: Eerdmans, 1996), 699, n. 13, which reads: "e.g., *1 Enoch* 93:5, 8; Philo, *Heir* 279 (Abraham); *Jub.* 21:24 (Isaac). Most commentators take this position [that the root refers to the patriarchs]; cf., e.g., Chrysostom; Godet; Cranfield; Fitzmyer."

18. Note that the verse does *not* say "enemies of God" but only "enemies"— of the gospel. There is almost no verse in which the Jewish people are described as God's enemies, unless Paul is here thinking of Isaiah 63:10: "Yet they rebelled and grieved his Holy Spirit. So he turned and became their enemy and he himself fought against them," an unusual usage. In any event, those translations that use the phrase "enemies of God" in Romans 11:28 have added "of God," which does not appear in the Greek.

## Chapter 8: A Pentecost Meditation: How to Anticipate Christ's Return

1. See W. E. Vine, *Expository Dictionary of New Testament Words* (Grand Rapids: Zondervan, 1981 [reprint]), s.v. "Time." The distinction between the two terms is not cut-and-dried. Compare comments by Richard N. Longenecker, "Acts," 256, in *Expositor's Bible Commentary*, vol. 9 (Grand Rapids: Zondervan, 1981); F. F. Bruce, *The Book of the Acts*, rev. ed., New International Commentary on the New Testament (Grand Rapids: Eerdmans, 1988), 35, n. 29.

2. Edgar C. Whisenant, *88 Reasons Why the Rapture Could Be in 1988*.

## Chapter 9: The Countdown Commission

1. See http://www.jewsforjesus.org/answers/prophecy for interesting and helpful information on this subject.

## Appendix B: A Christian Shavuot (Pentecost) Celebration

1. Available in *Hosanna! Music Songbook, Volume 6* (Intergity's Hosanna! Music can be ordered through Integrity Media, 800-533-6912; product #HMSB06). Congregations that are members of CCLI can access the lyrics through CCLI's Web site, song #187056. The song can also be heard on the album *Up to Zion* by Paul Wilbur, available through Purple Pomegranate Productions at http://store.jewsforjesus.org/ppp/product.php?prodid=77.

2. Congregations that are members of CCLI can access the lyrics through CCLI's Web site, song #14301.

3. Congregations that are members of CCLI can access the lyrics through CCLI's Web site, song #20546.

## Appendix D: Law, Grace, and Tradition

1. The Navigators have helpfully published Calvin's "Three Uses of the Law" at http://www.navpress.com/EPubs/DisplayArticle/1/1.21.4.html.

# INDEX

# ACKNOWLEDGMENTS

**W**e want to thank the Lord for all those who had a hand in this book. To those on the Jews for Jesus staff who faithfully attended our study sessions asking many probing questions, your insights and encouragement are much appreciated. For her contribution, Ruth Rosen should be added as a co-author, but there wasn't enough room on the book cover. Thanks for Pastor Joe Fuiten of Cedar Park Assembly for your enthusiasm and for the helpful material you contributed. We are grateful also for the critical contributions of Dr. William Raccah and Dr. Harold Hoehner, who each read over the manuscript and provided important corrections and added refinement. Last but not least, thanks to our editor Pam Pugh, who once again did a masterful job of pulling all the loose ends together and pushing us through to the finish line.

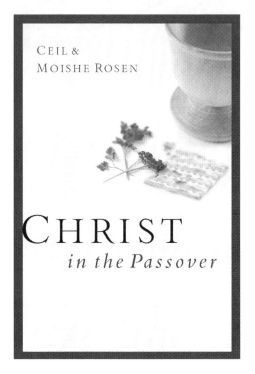

CEIL &
MOISHE ROSEN

# CHRIST
*in the Passover*

ISBN-10: 0-8024-1389-7
ISBN-13: 978-0-8024-1389-5

To prepare for Passover, why must all leaven—that which "puffs up" dough—be put away? Which of the four Passover cups was Jesus holding when He said, "Do this in remembrance of Me"? And what do His words "I am the gate" have to do with a blood-sealed door centuries before His time on earth? The basics of Passover may be familiar, but there is deeper meaning in the symbolism of this ancient yet contemporary celebration. *Christ in the Passover* is an appealing read that explains why "this night is different."

ISBN-10: 0-8024-1396-X
ISBN-13: 978-0-8024-1396-3

Why was it at the Feast of Tabernacles that Jesus said, "I am the Light of the World" and "Come to me and drink"? In the early days this festival was celebrated by erecting temporary shelters to demonstrate the transience of life; over the years meaningful new practices were added. You'll find *Christ in the Feast of Tabernacles* an intriguing read as you learn how the elements of this joyful and prophetic festival come together while Jesus both tabernacles with us now and is preparing an everlasting tabernacle for those who love Him.